Living in Language

Living in Language

International reflections
for the practising poet

Edited by Erica Hesketh

poetry
translation
centre

First published in 2024 by the Poetry Translation Centre Ltd
The Albany, Douglas Way, London, SE8 4AG

www.poetrytranslation.org

ISBN: 978-1-7398948-5-6

A catalogue record for this book is available from the British Library

Typeset in Minion Pro / Apple SD Gothic Neo / Arial Unicode MS /
Heiti TC / Helvetica / Hiragino Kaku Gothic Pro
by Poetry Translation Centre Ltd

Cover Design: Bern Roche Farrelly

Printed in the UK by T.J. Books Limited

The Poetry Translation Centre is supported using public funding
by Arts Council England.

Contents

Foreword   9
by Erica Hesketh

PART ONE: PERSPECTIVES ON POETRY

'At the Beginning of the Poem'   14

To Write, for the Poet, is to Engrave Upon Eternity,   16
   Then Perish in the Flesh Too Soon for Glory
by Gabriel *Mwènè* Okoundji

Life's Literary Stopping Places   20
by Karin Karakaşlı

Embracing the Gnarled Ineffable   27
by Habib Tengour

Poetry Practices Being Caught in the Act   34
by Lee Hyemi

'A Hidden Bird'   38

The Poem Chooses Its Own Birth   40
by Mohan Rana

PART TWO: MAKING POEMS

The Archaeology of Sound   50
by Bejan Matur

Substantial Words: Mastering the Gabay   57
by Asha Lul Mohamud Yusuf

Mythology As Metaphor   64
by Diana Anphimiadi

'Medusa'   72

Take the Poem-Shaped Bits Out of the Poems   74
by Yu Yoyo

A Wave Collapes On Another Wave   79
by Al-Saddiq Al-Raddi

Nightmare Inspiration   84
by Yang Lian

'Poems On Turning Back History *(for Hong Kong)*'   88

PART THREE: ON LANGUAGE

Living in Translation (excerpt)   92
by Laura Wittner

On Translation: Two Letters and a Reflection   99
by Ursula K Le Guin and Diana Bellessi

i-juca piranha   110
by Érica Zingano

The Calling to Write Poetry in an Indigenous Language 119
by Victor Terán

'Feast of the Dead'   128

PART THREE: SUBJECT AND CONTEXT

On Tanka Form   132
by Karan Kurose

A Poem on My Gravestone: On Death, Being   141
    Minang, and First Love
by Zar Mose

No Man Is a Fern Plant: Writing in Isolation   148
by Carla Diacov

Echoes of Love: Exploring Somali Literature   153
    and Personal Revelations
by Xasan Daahir Ismaaciil 'Weedhsame'

'Sucking the Stone'   160

Writing as a Woman; Or, Being a Woman Makes   162
    You Frown
by Legna Rodríguez Iglesias

A City Called Exile   167
by Azita Ghahreman

About the contributors   174

About the Poetry Translation Centre   188

Foreword

Erica Hesketh

If you are a poet, this book is for you. If you are a reader of poetry, this book is for you. If you are interested in how poetry is made around the world, in languages other than English, in the present day, this book is definitely for you!

Living in Language brings together reflections on poetry by leading poets from Asia, Africa and Latin America who write in a language other than English. Within these pages you'll find thoughts on the process of writing poems, from first inspirations to putting together a collection and beyond, by award-winning poets such as Bejan Matur (Turkey) and Al-Saddiq Al-Raddi (Sudan). You'll find illuminating pieces on non-western poetic forms by Asha Lul Mohamud Yusuf (Somaliland) and Karan Kurose (Japan), as well as essays on identifying your voice and honing your words on the page by Mohan Rana (India) and Lee Hyemi (South Korea). And you'll find plenty of newly translated poems to inspire you in your own practice.

However, this is not a how-to book; there are no writing prompts or tips on finding a publisher. Instead it is a book that turns towards questions of great importance: What is it to write about the female body, or from inside one (Legna Rodríguez Iglesias, Cuba)? What does it mean to be 'in exile' as a poet (Azita Ghahreman, Iran)? Who are your literary forebears, and are they different to mine (Gabriel *Mwènè* Okoundji, Republic of Congo)? What if your body isn't safe in the world – what does that do to your poems (Zar Mose, Indonesia)? What is the relationship between poetry and the truth (Habib Tengour, Algeria)? What are your poetic obsessions (Yang Lian, China)? How does it feel to write in isolation (Carla Diacov, Brazil)? What is a poetic 'journey' (Karin Karakaşlı, Turkey)? Why do poets the world over reach for mythological archetypes (Diana Anphimiadi, Georgia)? What is 'craft' and how do you avoid showing it (Yu Yoyo, China)? Where is the space for male vulnerability in poetry (Weedhsame, Somaliland)? And what if everything about your art is political, from the subject matter to the language you choose to write in (Victor Terán, Mexico)?

This collection of remarkable pieces on the craft and purpose of poetry marks the 20th birthday of the Poetry Translation Centre. Since 2004, when it was founded by the poet Sarah Maguire (1957–2017), the PTC has championed poetry from Asia, Africa and Latin America through collaborative translation workshops, dual-language poetry collections and lively poet tours across the UK. We have been lucky enough to meet and work with poets who are megastars in their own countries; poets forced into exile because of their art or activism; older poets who have inspired multiple generations with their work; and younger poets at the vanguard of new poetic movements. It has been a privilege to reconnect with so many of them to put together this book.

Translating their poems over the years has, we believe, expanded what is possible in poetry in English, through the introduction of new poetic forms, ideas and styles – new ways of doing things. Our translation workshops have been a haven of mutual respect and creativity, as well as an energetic source of brand-new English translations; there are now over 600 translated poems available to read for free on the PTC website. And I wish you could bottle the feeling when a poem is read aloud at an event, in its original language and in translation – the moment when a poem from one place is held by a room full of people in another, when poetry itself becomes a shared space in which people from different backgrounds and perspectives can meet. I guess that magic bottle would be labelled 'The opposite of war', a phrase often used by Sarah to describe the act of translating poetry.

Of course, none of this would be possible without the many, many brilliant translators we have worked with since 2004, several of whom have translated pieces for this anthology. Translation is a creative act which is inherently political, and radical in both senses: it offers us a way to imagine entirely different worlds, and it reaches carefully down to the roots of a text to carry it, leafy and vibrant, to a new home in a new language. Translators are artists, stewards and advocates all rolled into one, and deserve much more recognition. In this book you'll find a few reflections on the practice of translation itself, including thoughts on craft and graft by Argentine poet Laura Wittner, an exclusive excerpt from a work-in-progress by Brazilian poet Érica Zíngano, and an exchange of letters between Argentine poet Diana Bellessi and American writer Ursula K Le Guin, who became friends by translating each other's poetry.

It should go without saying, but unfortunately can't yet, that the readership or 'market' of poetry in this country is not a homogenous block of monolingual English-speakers; millions of us speak more than one language and have heritage from elsewhere. Since 2004 the PTC has worked to challenge the notions of 'us' and 'them' when it comes to poetry, and literature in general. The diverse poets we have championed may be 'foreign' to some audiences, but are very much 'ours' to the many well-established diaspora communities, and immigrants (like myself), who call this place home.

Whatever your own starting point, thank you so much for picking up this book. I hope that you enjoy spending time with the reflections. I hope that you find among them a few new poets to call 'yours', and that they offer you inspiration and encouragement for your own writing – whatever form, direction or language it takes – for years to come.

London, January 2024

Part One:
Perspectives on Poetry

AU COMMENCEMENT DU POÈME

Okundji, Pampou, Ampili,
                    Ndzama,
                            Apanga,

Epouki, Kélonangako,
        et vous autres oncles, pères et mères,
        que ma bouche manque ici de nommer :

                    Par votre présence
                        je sens en moi
                        au jour le jour, à la nuit la nuit
                        comme une soif d'être homme, encore.

            Ompuhà oli ma bè,
        lé nà mwana odumwahà !
    Mè a mbalàhà ma bè atsù mvouori, atsù mvouori.

Ankamà mà'antsini, andouoni mà adzwuidzè !
            Ndà kali, ndà kali !
            Okè okè, dzwè lè yè !

                                    Gabriel *Mwènè* Okoundji

14

AT THE BEGINNING OF THE POEM

Okundji, Pampou, Ampili,
        Ndzama,
                Apanga,

Epouki, Kélonangako,
        and all you other uncles, fathers and mothers,
        whom my mouth fails to name here:

                By your presence
                I sense in me
                from day to day, from night to night
                like a thirst to be man, again.

        Ompuhà oli ma bè,
    lé nà mwana odumwahà!
Mè a mbalàhà ma bè atsù mvouori, atsù mvouori.

Ankamà mà'antsini, andouoni mà adzwuidzè!
        Ndà kali, ndà kali!
        Okè okè, dzwè lè yè!

                        Translated by Delaina Haslam

To Write, for the Poet, is to Engrave Upon Eternity, Then Perish in the Flesh Too Soon for Glory

Gabriel *Mwènè* Okoundji

Translated from the French by Delaina Haslam

Poetry is tune, rhythm and cadence, stretching in space to life's margins. As Hölderlin said on the banks of the Garonne: *Poets establish that which endures.*[1] I agree with this. Even though I am aware that I am not yet a poet and will never be one, despite writing for many years.

Man remains, throughout his existence, an apprentice when faced with Creation. Life is an offering; it is not a gift. It is a mysterious, enduring and immense offering, at once simple, at once multiple, never monotonous, always mutable, sometimes veiled, sometimes hidden; but whose puzzles and wonders are refreshed every morning so that no living being – not even a poet – can conquer it entirely.

No human can find fulfilment when empty. As an apprentice poet I was nourished by the fathers of Négritude, with Aimé Césaire as their figurehead; by the elders of Congolese literature, with Tati Loutard at its golden peak; at the banquet of the Surrealists, with Breton, Ducasse and Char bound close to my soul; by Musset,

---

1   From the poem 'Andenken' ('Remembrance'), translated from the German by James Mitchell.

Mayakovsky, Jabesh, Pessoa, Tagore, Asturias, Manciet, Lahor, Juarroz, Santoka, Neruda, Hesiod, Dante and Lonnröt. They are all watchmen, movement sensors in the infinite sky, the cosmic abyss.

My illustrious guides taught me this: Across every inch of the earth, the poem is never wrong to be a poem. And so, along the way, the apprentice poet in me recalled the stars of Mount Amaya, where – beneath the light of the Teke cosmogony – the transmission of the speech magnifies the eloquence of the word-bearers.

Among those word-bearers, those noble speakers of the essential, was my aunt-mother[2] Ampili, the storyteller. *A straight word does not turn away*, she would say.

There was Pampou, the man who shakes the forest to the rhythm of his step, the venerable magus with a voice as tender as the great love of living souls, and luminous as the dawn. *All roads start from emotion and lead to emotion: Rome is just a call along the way!* he would declare.

They are my source; and as every source is destined for the apogee of its flow, they would murmur in my ear, those two messengers.

Every mortal who receives such a transmission must learn to live, from day to day, from night to night, in harmony with their world without seeking to dominate it. Where the mind is free, the heart is fearless, and harmony is perfect.

---

2   Translator's note: For the Teke people, as for many Central African populations, society is organised matrilineally, with all children belonging to the mother's lineage. All children call their maternal aunts 'mother'. Ampili was the older sister of Gabriel's mother. Since it was Ampili who brought him up, she thereby became his natural mother, with greater value than his biological mother. Since this may be difficult to understand for readers outside the culture, he created this compound noun, aunt-mother.

Ampili and Pampou did not possess the writing of the language, but they held the essentials: the proverb, the tale, the adage that teaches the proud – who believe they know everything – to unlearn their knowledge; the maxim that constantly reminds us that no one in the world has a monopoly on life; the ending of the chanted myth, which teaches that only love makes us brave, and whoever knows this does not fight; the motto which states that if a dispute becomes inevitable between two beings, the one who regrets wins; the saying that everything under the sky aspires to balance, that excess on earth is never good in a human life.

It is they, Ampili and Pampou, who are my initiators. It is they who speak in my poems; I only dance to the rhythm of their chants. I am only an interpreter of their voice. I only nod my head as I listen – for it is said that when the ear hears a word of truth, the head cannot help but agree.

It is they, Ampili and Pampou, who led me to the clear realisation that written thought is all too often silent. That is why I consider myself an orator, an apprentice poet, with a pen in my hand.

An orator-initiate who has been led to believe that the words of the poem are the type that heal the soul's pain and right the mind's error.

An apprentice poet who bows down before the manifest truth: since the heart beats in the language of emotion, then emotion is our first skin, our first cell, our first blood, our first neuron. The depth of the poetic song is boundless in the territory of emotion.

An orator-initiate for whom the poem's chant fans the flame. However, the poet does not speak the world, does not show it, does not teach it; the poet signals, and that is all. And whoever listens to the signal that blooms from the murmur of a line is not alienated, but keeps the scope to enjoy the freedom of being in the world.

The apprentice poet in me knows how precious the poem is. It is, of all earth's creations, what will remain to humans when everything has been expressed.

And I am the proof made flesh that the poet is above all an initiate: initiation being the path that reveals the true words hiding in our speech, so that Man learns in his daily existence to trust in the inherent vulnerability of all living beings. And every initiate knows – having learned this – that the whole world rests in the lap of an ant.

And so I live by the word of my two masters, Ampili and Pampou. Their language is the only one I can truly speak. They are the ones who made my heart beat towards an abundance of emotion. It is their speech which ripens in my veins and in my belly.

Finally, to close, I admit to being someone who thinks that life is painful only at the outer edges of poetry. This is an act of faith.

However, I am aware that what is true for one Man is not true for all.

Life's Literary Stopping Places

Karin Karakaşlı

Translated from the Turkish by Ayça Türkoğlu

For me, literature is a looping journey; I have passed each of its stops many times, never tiring of any of them. But if I must have a beginning, then it had better be language itself.

I grew up bilingual. Before writing or literature, there was language. Words and sound. A child's home is the limit of their world at first, and the child believes that the language they speak at home is the language the whole world speaks. And so it was for me. One day, I heard different voices on the street. There were different voices coming out of the TV too, which in those days would broadcast very short, black-and-white programmes. I turned to my grandmother, who had taught me my own voice. 'Yaya,' I said. 'What is this?' 'It's Turkish,' she said. My next question naturally followed: 'Then what do we speak?' 'We speak Armenian, sweetheart,' she said, smiling. The two languages were labelled like jam jars that day, and that was the day I split in two.

Then came school with its differently coloured book covers. My Armenian exercise book had a blue cover and my Turkish book had a red one. If that weren't enough, letters had begun raining down on me from the sky. I had 38 Armenian letters, like hieroglyphs, and 29 Turkish letters from the Latin alphabet. I had two languages in my dreams at night, in my unending daydreams, and in the games I played out in the street. I was too much.

I will never forget the day I moved on from picture books to books filled with text. In the blink of an eye, I could see pictures in my imagination in the space between two sentences. I was no longer in that little living room with the grating over the window. I was floating in the air, free of time and space, just as I wanted. I was breathless in the face of the book's magical power. And it was while I was reading that I first felt the enormity of writing. Literature became my freedom, first through reading, and then by writing the books I dreamed of reading myself.

Being bilingual is like being at the cinema and constantly being able to change the camera angle and focus. You become an inner eye and an outer eye at the same time. You're able to look upon what's closest to you from a distance, and look up close at things that are far away. Armenian has its own alphabet, harking back to ancient times. It has allowed me to share that world's hidden stories. It has also nourished me in the literary language I established in Turkish, with its music, its rhythm, and its deep-rooted writing tradition.

But language is not merely a conduit, it is a subject that exerts its own will. A language can choose you. German, the first foreign language I learned, was freedom for me; it opened the door to a whole new region of culture, and I became so saturated in it that it became another language I can write in. I still take great pleasure in expanding the scope of my linguistic playground by learning new languages, and in my ability to take refuge in parallel universes when the world feels too small.

With language as its main ingredient, literature presents a different kind of challenge to other artforms. We use the same language to live our everyday lives, to fight, to swear, to command others to torture, or commit massacres. The power of words is great. Words can be a weapon that kills, but they can also heal. It's the intention that matters. So, I fuss over the literary language I have built. I never skimp on giving it the care and the effort it deserves. I'm a steadfast worker, a patient collector, a compulsive observer. I'm not always tightly bound to life. Death is always close by. But I am in love with life itself, with its infinite existence that transcends the human span, with every fibre of my being.

It always seemed to me that literature and life meet at the thin line of horizon between the sky and the sea. Sometimes I can't tell where one ends and the other begins. Sometimes the storm is at sea, and sometimes all hell breaks loose in the sky. They rise and fall like a seesaw, literature and life.

When I set out to write all this, and more, when I pour life into literature's mould, I pause for a moment at the beginning. The truth is that everything has accumulated long before the pen touches the pages of your notebook, before your fingers move across the keys, and then it's time for it to flow. And as it flows, you have to drift along with it. You look down and your words have begun writing you.

Whether it's yourself you're facing, or some imaginary being, writing always means searching for your interlocutor, extricating it from yourself, and sharing it. You will be the one who begins and the one who brings it to an end. You're free of dimensions, free of shackles, as free as you can be. Yet in that freedom there's a responsibility, too. If there's one thing I've learned, it's that literature cannot compete with the fiction of life. Sometimes the reality of life is so absurd that if I tried to write it, people would say, 'Well, she's embellished that.' But there's another thing I know, deep in my bones: literature begins where life leaves off. While life is busy being lived, literature is the record-keeper of what it is and what it cannot be. It seems to me that when life forgets itself, it looks to literature to remember.

I think literature is inherently oppositional. Why would you stop living your own life and set about creating other worlds, unless you had some problem or some inescapable purpose? For my part, I've always been passionate about literature's ability to record alternatives to official history and to liberate the human story. I've taken particular strength from seeking out the voices of those condemned to silence for different reasons. I find it meaningful to create different universes, to dream up dimensionless worlds, and to push the possibilities of language to their absolute limits. In doing this, I pursue a truth which either some power has deprived us of, or which we daren't look in the eye. There is something tragic and telling about the fact that we are still drowning in lies even now that channels of communication are so numerous and varied. When everything and everyone is telling lies, literature will continue to express the truth of a person, a history, a geography, a future. I write this with real faith.

One of the most magical aspects of writing is that every genre is a school in itself.

Stories are my first love, a secret garden where I photograph life's milestones, creating scenes like those in the films I love, and where I touch the soul in its barest state; stories are an alternative universe I slip into, before allowing the reader to join me. Novels are life itself, a contract for stability and permanence. They are an adventure I embark on, following my heroes, and the adventure doesn't end until they say so. Essays and columns are the battlefield where I try to record day-to-day life, laying claim to the truth that is being taken from us and appropriated. They are a sanctuary with different doors, an ocean that takes me in and allows me to become one of its atoms when I'm spilling from life's edges. The deeper I dive, the clearer it is, the further I go, the closer it is. With its authenticity in dialogue, its discipline which doesn't permit even the slightest hole in plot development, its test of sincerity, and its realism, which doesn't compromise on hope, children's literature is the school I attend with utmost joy.

*

Poetry is my final stop.

I was brave enough to read poems early, but I was late in summoning the courage to write them. To me, poetry has always been an anomalous, singular universe within literature itself. It's a force that shakes me, envelops me. When I feel incapable of doing anything, I reach instinctively for a poetry book. If I haven't spoken to anyone all day, even if I've barely heard my own voice, I'll mutter a poem to myself gently. Poetry brings me back to myself.

As a reader, I think I owe a lot to poetry in translation. As far as I'm concerned, nothing matches the nature of poetry the way translation does, because poetry has an inherent need to be on the move all the time. It must be spoken time and time again, echoed in other languages. Translation is its greatest companion on that journey.

You might say that poetry translation is a crossroads in the realm of interlingual relations; where one language goes, carried by poetry, another language rises to meet it. Poetry translation multiplies the creativity in all languages, infinitely expanding the possibilities. As the form closest to oral literature and music, poetry inhabits a special and permeable place in all of humanity's languages. Poetry has a magic to it akin to the myths and archetypes we view as our common cultural heritage. I often try to translate poems in other languages that strike me into Turkish. When I do this, I first have to get some distance from the source text, because translation is a state of limbo. Cut adrift from two worlds, I find myself swaying in the void and wanting to become a bridge between the two.

At the very end of all these stops, I eventually found a description of the poem I wanted to write, in a poem by the 20th-century Greek poet Yannis Ritsos. He said:

I believe in poetry, in love, in death,
which is precisely why I believe in immortality. I write a verse,
I write the world; I exist; the world exists.
A river flows from the tip of my little finger.
The sky is seven times blue. This purity
is once again the prime truth, my last will.[1]

To me, poetry is a propulsive love in terms of its economy of language, its creativity with metaphors, its intensity, its inner harmony and music. It's the empty space where I feel free in the truest sense, the place I run to when I'm afraid.

The power of being able to write about your vulnerabilities is inexplicable. The voices of everyone who has experienced that same humbling reverberate brokenly in your words. As you heal, you grow stronger, and as you share, you recover. Life is augmented when you make the voiceless speak, when you grasp the history of a geography from its truth, and talk about worlds visible only to you. Ultimately, literature is always seeking an interlocutor, people who, come the morning, will read the words you wrote on lonely nights with trembling hands. You hope that what you write makes a difference; that you dare to attempt what has never before been done with the power of words, to inform decisions which should have been taken long ago. To create a before and after. To leave a mark. To touch.

Poetry is our companion from our first breath, the first sound we make, the first word that leaves our lips. It's what we commit to memory, our world of imagination, a treasure that has existed, and will continue to exist, forever. A poem can start a revolution and bring love to a gentle end. You can mourn your loved ones with poetry and make your children's hearts soar with it. I don't consider rows of lines filled with heroic rhetoric to be poetry. Poetry is the main vein that feeds literature of every genre. It

1 Translated from the Greek by N.C. Germanacos.

enables us to remember the importance of music, of rhythm, to rediscover each time the power of form, of metaphor and imagery. Stories specific to certain cultures make the singularity of the human experience, shaped as it is by language, part of a universal adventure. Poetry existed before writing and it will be with humanity until it takes its last breath. And even after that, it will continue its existence in the wind, in the waves, in the glow of a supernova in the emptiness of space.

Poetry is the only place where I can step beyond the boundaries of time and space, where I can be completely free. I call it a fragile force. Poetry needs no purpose to exist; its existence brings its own meaning. We would live far emptier lives without its raw compassion. It is all-encompassing in its possibilities; it can tell a story, it can set a cinematic scene, take on an epic voice, or emulate a song. It can become a manifesto in itself and ignite a revolution. It cries out the stories of hidden history, laying bare the spirit of a geography, of a people. It can touch the very heart of a secret that you can only whisper when you're alone.

The limitless possibilities that poetry presents in terms of language, style, and form are almost equal to the omnipotence of life itself. As I've said, it always seemed to me that literature and life meet at the thin line of horizon between the sea and the sky. Poetry is that horizon.

When I feel like an exile in my homeland, a refugee in the world, poetry is my only home. It grants me the opportunity for defiance as much as solace. It teaches me to dare to be brave with my fear, to fear with bravery. I pick up the pieces of myself, greater in their brokenness than they are as a whole, and I strike out again.

Embracing the Gnarled Ineffable

Habib Tengour

Translated from the French by Delaina Haslam

My mother tongue is Algerian Arabic. Being born in the colonial period, I was educated in French. Only in Qur'anic school were we permitted to learn Arabic. This school was more like a nursery where we learned the sacred text by heart without really understanding the language. This did not teach us to go on to write in Arabic, but we were nevertheless able to absorb the language and retain its rhythm and sounds. So when I started to write, it was in French. Kateb Yacine, Mohammed Dib and Mouloud Feraoun had paved the way for me. I could lean on them to learn to write. They translated their spoken words into French – a 'perfect' French so that they would be recognized as writers. But their literary language plays with dialectal Arabic, Tamazight and oral culture without being exotic. This makes their French unusual.

In truth, I was not completely comfortable at first, and I felt guilty for not being able to write in my mother tongue. However, since my need to write was strong, I gradually shook off the guilt. It took me a long time to understand that all writing is in effect translating our mother tongue and the language learned at school to create our own language; for me it has meant finding a way for my Arabic to echo beneath the school-learned French in my writing.

*

After my first attempts at writing in 1962, when Algeria had just gained independence following a harrowing war of liberation, I felt a pressing need to translate the experience of my people and the reality around me, without sensation or embellishment. It was Victor Hugo who infected me with the writing virus. Reading *Les Orientales*, I rediscovered the *Mu'allaqāt*, which I'd heard in childhood, recited by my father. Nerval's *Voyage to the Orient* and Baudelaire's *Les paradis artificiels* brought other images and sounds back to me that I'd heard as a child. Reading, reading, reading (I read a lot).

Reading these texts, I believed in the Writer as witness of his age, borne by his people, and bearer of an unheard truth – the expression of a singular 'me' and a collective conscience. I dreamed of producing a lament which voiced, soothed and amplified the suffering and the struggle endured by my country under colonisation. It took all my youth and ambition to dare to do so.

Later, reading Joyce and the Surrealist poets disorientated me completely and forced me to revise my conception of writing. For what and for whom to write became idle, useless questions; the only thing that mattered was the *fact* of writing, of methodically exploring all its intricacies without complacency – to grasp the complexity of a moving and unfamiliar reality. The language of my writing was no longer the issue, even though it remained one since injunctions issued by the authorities made it obligatory to write only in the 'national language'.

*

In truth, this need to record 'the real', whatever the method used, is at the very foundation of poetic speech, being as it is free from any form of fiction. It's not about imitating reality. The poet pays attention to the power of words to say things, taking care not to overuse them; the poet sounds out the repercussions of a phrase; the poet ensures the unveiling of reality through non-speculative language. Writing poetry makes demands on language in terms of exploring the sonority of resonances and the sequencing of images. It links meaning and sound to produce the unexpected. Poets serve their people by devoting themselves to their writing. This commitment cannot be ordered by a political power. The poet imposes it on him or herself, following Baudelaire:

> This fire burns our brains so fiercely, we wish to plunge
> To the abyss' depths, Heaven or Hell, does it matter?
> To the depths of the Unknown to find something new![1]

The entire pursuit of the poem – a subtle weaving alongside the clamour of the crowd – is a crossing into exile. All that is discovered is unknown. The poet must break new ground to (re)find the meaning of words.

'Poetry is absolute reality. [...] The more poetic something is, the truer it is.' I used these words by Novalis as the epigraph to my 1983 poetic work *La vieux de la montagne*. I thereby assigned to my poetic approach the task of unveiling the real, of 'embracing gnarled reality' as Rimbaud proclaimed on his descent in *A Season in Hell*. A difficult task. I have not yet despaired of finding the 'method' to achieve it.

Poetry connects language with the body of the poet so that words appear in all their aptness and exactness. In my case, this connection is coupled with the difficulty of translating this reality into the language of the conqueror (the French I learnt in compulsory education) – my mother tongue, dialectal Arabic, being confined to orality. Poetry thus remains a way of working on myself and on reality, which it incorporates in writing; somehow it engenders it, and this is why poetry is reality.

*

My research as an anthropologist similarly consists of recording observed reality and examining the workings of orality, but

1   From 'The Voyage', translated from French by William Aggeler.

the academic approach has always seemed to me ill-equipped to reveal the profound truth of things beyond their reality – to understand them not only intellectually but also empathetically. This is why much of my anthropological research on ageing in exile, traditional culture, and the popular imagination and orality have served my poetry more than they have my academic publications.

However, whether in academic research or poetic process, the profound truth of reality remains ineffable. While sociological and anthropological investigation gives me a general understanding of the phenomena studied, poetry helps me to find the right words and original expressions; it prevents me from straying onto the well-trodden ground of the layman I remain; it ensures the precision of my lens. Taking a poetic approach places me within the subject matter and simultaneously at a distance. I try to correctly apprehend reality, both lived and observed, and to record it without extraneous effects. The poetic word speaks of reality as closely as possible without speaking it fully.

Academic research reconstructs reality and theorises it to expose methods of action. Poetry lets us dismantle and exhibit the machinery of this construction and reorganise it with no explicit methodological aim. Writing poetry is always a matter of deconstruction and reconstruction of the linguistic structure suggested by the surrounding reality. It is not a matter of transforming reality but of showing it differently; it must be pronounced yet not flagrantly imposed on the text. The reading of the poem must allow a rewriting to let in other visions of reality.

The pre-Modernist novel required reconstruction in the name of a fictional continuity, while poetry delivers it in fragmentation. Reality is never given in linear writing, but rather in its discontinuity; its perception can only be fragmentary. The poem's grasp of reality is a matter of confrontation, collage, editing, metaphor, rhythm, and the meeting of images, sounds, and objects that are not meant to meet; these encounters drive the poem and make us wonder what we see in reality. This is not objective reality, but rather its reorganisation due to chance: the 'objective chance' of the selection. Reality can be read in a thousand and one ways. The poet is also careful to record and incorporate all the facts he sees. His eye/(his body) captures these while his mind interrogates them; and the clashes which thereby result produce *Illuminations*.

Reality, which is itself in pieces, is discovered in a proliferation of languages. It does not let itself be understood in the clarity of continuous discourse. What the poet translates is often a stuttering. As far as translation is concerned, the fragment captures reality in its immediacy. These are scraps that the poet reorganises to produce something – something different that is not reality as it happened but a reality still in the making. The way these fragments of reality are entangled gives another reality. This reality is never fully produced; each time, these fragments – for those who will read or hear them – can produce different realities because the words, depending on the emphasis placed on this or that sequence of the sentence, will produce something else that forces us to ask questions.

*

My writing questions reality and popular myths. Daring to enter into the myth – to break it if it has become petrified, or reorient it if it is still alive – is what makes me constantly re-read the *Odyssey*, the *Mu'allaqāt*, Islam, the history of the Algerian national movement, the class struggle, and so on. Myths are built collectively. I grew up in the myth of the war of national liberation – the Revolution, we called it. Not only the Algerian Revolution, but also the Russian Revolution, the French Revolution, the Chinese Revolution, the myth of the red flag. These are myths that give meaning to actions. The poetic text opens the doors of the myth and deconstructs it to reveal a reality. For the myth proposes a

31

false image of reality: one that is aesthetically beautiful, but which can seduce us and lead us to act in a certain way. The core of the issue for me is how to use poetry to rid the myth of the illusory image, to identify what is behind the mirage. It is multifaceted like a kaleidoscope, with many forms that will guide our gaze. It is an examination of the imagination: not simply my individual imagination, but a shared imagination.

Moreover, poetry reveals to each of us the resources of our humanity and of other higher truths. It is no coincidence that mystics of all religions, and especially Tasawwuf (Sufism), have expressed their ecstasy in poems that continue to move us deeply today. Religious fundamentalism is at odds with this approach. Fundamentalism, conversely, seeks to assert an indisputable truth; its vision is unshakable. But all visions must be shaken. Poetry is a moving perception of reality, a quiet instability. Instability is not non-stability; it is, on the contrary, very anchored in the movement of things. The poem never offers an image or sound as fully framed and complete; it offers threads which invite us to reconsider the image and sounds that the poet perceives and wishes to present in his own language. Depending on the moment and the way in which we pick up these threads ourselves, they give different representations and open our eyes and ears to something else – to a future, to the other. Quite the opposite of a dogmatic ideology. We need poetry in order to live in harmony with the world and to find ourselves in connections with others. Poetry is the intermediary which helps orient us.

*

Having been writing for so many years, I now accept what Abdallah Benanteur[2] always told me: artists serve their art, they

2   Abdallah Benanteur was an Algerian painter and engraver; born in Mostaganem on 3 March 1931, died 31 December 2017, Ivry-sur-Seine (France); an important figure in modern Algerian painting.

must not use it to serve themselves. They have nothing to wish for and nothing to worry about as to the reception of their work; they only have to do their best. To set about it, with modesty, each day, relentlessly.

Humbly serving writing in order to *reveal* what is beyond the presence of things instead of using it for other purposes seems to me today to be the only way to carry out a radical poetic practice. Any injunction external to the inner necessity to write can only distort the result. An approach that allows me to do my work in relative peace.

Poetry Practices Being Caught in the Act

Lee Hyemi

Translated from the Korean by Soje

> . . . we took our measure
> of just how admonishing time, alternately agonising and
> benumbing time, lent us so much but wrested more still.
> Even so, it left us transparent to ourselves
> and proffered us the milk of years to savour in warm bubbles
> when this milk very much was nourishing us . . .
>
> René Char tr. Jeffrey Zuckerman, 'Progeny of the Sun'

OPENING THE LID OF LANGUAGE

Poetry is the lunch box of language. It packs in human emotions like sorrow, ecstasy, bewilderment, love, fear, and the sublime for future generations, just as our bodies deliver the secret materials of the universe to a distant future through collections of DNA. We gather fleeting thoughts, feelings, moments, voices, and memories to launch beyond the horizon of our present in the unmanned rocket that is Poetry. Often I write poems imagining the precise moment a rocket of words reaches a future so distant that it enters outer space and travels across a distant spacetime. Words earn their bodies and come alive the moment they're written on paper. To live a life longer than that of who birthed them. A life with its mouth full of purpose.

Poetry reminds us of our transience. In my case, I feel a sense of inferiority around the sentences I've written. They will outlive me like graffiti, like echoes. Poetry is not immortal or fixed in place; it metamorphoses and reincarnates in the midst of continuous change. Isn't that why we continuously grasp at moments brushing by and attempt to affix the ephemeral to poetry? To revive them? In the way our physical existence moves through the birth-death cycle, poetry is change itself, born anew each time without any absolutes. Some poems are letters mailed to a future library. Some scribbles are cave paintings made by a single artist. Every diary is a will.

SECRETLY (OR GETTING CAUGHT) WINKING

Not long ago, I hid a love letter in a library book and wrote down the shelfmark number for my lover. I imagined them going to the library, searching for the book, and eventually reading my confessions inside a letter inside a book. Doesn't this stunt of mine – that is, hiding a juicy secret for eyes to glimpse behind the solid door of a book – resemble the writing of poetry? Amusingly, my lover mistook the shelfmark number for a flight number. And come to think of it, aeroplanes and books do both transport us to other worlds. My surprise gift may not have worked out as planned, but I was able to present a letter with time elapsed in its mouth.

Why did I risk hiding my letter somewhere unfamiliar to me and my lover? Let me tell you: to create a secret. In a covert act of solidarity and collusion. Baudelaire (translated by A.S. Kline) was right: 'What is tedious about love-making is that it is a crime where one cannot do without an accomplice.' The inexplicable bond between a writer and their reader has to do with this sedition. And so poetry gives hand signals, reads the room, plays tricks, holds back laughter. It is a train passing through a tunnel, an optical illusion. A stolen kiss.

I hid such playful winks throughout my poetry collection *Unexpected Vanilla*. I wanted to reconsider vanilla in its sense of the universal. Freaks, kinksters, queers, perverts, cuckolds, asexuals, monomaniacs, hedonists, et al. are often depicted as deviating from the 'universal human experience' despite being inextricable from our shared reality. But what is universal, versus what is special? What should we name the colours at the periphery of the spectrum of ultraviolet light? Every one of us wears socially prescribed universalities over each of our very personal and special bodies. *That* is the 'unexpected vanilla', where interior and exterior constantly collide and merge.

In particular, women's bodies are targeted as a battleground of ideologies. Their souls are trapped inside bodies plastered with bright-red stickers: sexual objectification, labour exploitation, reproductive coercion, total domination. I hope the poems I meet help me go beyond these social constraints and allow bodies to exist as they please.

FLOWING TOWARD THE UNKNOWN

Instead of knowing the future we were gifted music instead Like how we come to know a time and gather to give form to the world Like how thoughts intertwine and crumble and become a sentence at last

– Lee Hyemi tr. Soje, 'Mm' in *Scarcookie*

As three-dimensional beings existing in time, we create meaning by travelling between what we do not know and what we already know. When we listen to music, for example, we connect the musical notes we just heard to what came before, and anticipate the notes we might hear. This complex process takes place in an instant, but has a clear sequence. Listening to music shows a will to fully experience each moment and illuminate our stock-still world as if to decorate a Christmas tree.

In short, we can experience music because we can both exist *in* time and travel *through* time.

Like music, poetry is a temporal art, of moving toward the unknown while recognizing the pre-existing meaning, because literature cannot be understood without remembering the word or phrase that comes before it. Without carrying one's memory into the unknown. It is a law of time and much like the progression of our lives. People often say that 'time passes', but it's actually people who pass by. To us time appears to be in motion because everything except time passes. Like the view from a moving train, we start from the present and move toward the continuous future. Like an endless relay race, the past delivers the baton of memory to the present, the present to the next, and the present after that to the one after that, from which the next present emerges. Poetry is born in the moment we take the baton.

Writers and readers of poetry are athletes of the mind, Olympians of their mother tongues. People train in a primary language and experiment with the potential their language can acquire and expand inside their bodies throughout their lives. Writers, then, are more like professional athletes in that they do this more consciously. What's more, poets of a lesser spoken language (unlike English) must consider the potential of specificity in addition to the universality and truth of their language, with translation in mind. It's a question of how far one can use one's language to explore the possibilities of the world.

To steal sentences from time and hide them in a library is to wink at one's future lover or reader, don't you think? Like children playing hide-and-seek, meanings giggle as they hide themselves between shelves of the unknown and the familiar. To communicate without communicating. To be caught more compellingly and ever so beautifully.

숨은 새

책장을 넘기며
날개를 꺼낸다

어두운 페이지를 깨트려
주어진 여백을 따라

갈피의 빛을 배웠지
펼치면 달아나는
새의 기척을

작은 속삭임에도 눈가를 물들이던
떨림의 주파수를

숨은 우리가 창조한 공기의 단위
투명하게 펄럭이는 깃발이었어

좋아해
발아진 소리를 주고받으며
여기를 만들어내는 모험을
오래 머금어 깊숙해진
부름을

책이 수많은 빈틈으로 이루어진 건축이라면
접힌 그늘만큼의 부피를 품어 안겠지

공중을 안쪽으로 당겨 앉히기 위해
호흡의 태엽이 조금씩 감기는 지금

엎질러진 의미들이
손가락을 딛고 날아간다

속삭여봐
호수를 은빛으로 채점하는 물수제비처럼

사이에서 자라난 낱말들이
새로운 방향을 얻도록

무수히 깃털을 내어놓으며
틈새를 태어나게 하는 휘황으로

Lee Hyemi

A HIDDEN BIRD

Turning the pages
we unfold our wings

having broken the dark to follow
margins given to us

having learned the light of instinct
the sound of a bird that escapes
as we spread open

the frequency of tremors
that tear from sweet nothings

having created a unit of air called breath
a flag that waves invisibly

We love
the romp of creating space
through call and response
a call deepened
by time

If books are an architecture of openings
they must embrace every folded shadow

Breaths slowly wind
inviting air inside

as spilled meanings
step on fingers to fly away

Why don't you whisper
like a stone that skips forth silvering a lake

so words bubbling in between
may find new lines

toward a luminosity that is an opening
freeing untold feathers

Translated by Soje

The Poem Chooses Its Own Birth

Mohan Rana

Translated from the Hindi by Sarabjeet Garcha

In a wordless spacetime, I make windows of poetry. After many years of writing poems, I feel as if I am a transparent paper-window in the walls of memory, a window bearing words written with water.

*

I did not aspire to be or become a poet. Never in my wildest dreams had I fancied myself writing poems. I neither thought about nor ever read poems with much enthusiasm. As a teenager, I was more interested in reading novels. I didn't choose poetry; it chose me. I only had curiosity, which suddenly became a butterfly and fluttered away. I was only a cocoon. So, how did all of this happen? How did I step into the circle of poetry? When and how did I start writing poems? The pivotal event which altered the course of my life had slipped my own mind until I sat down to write this essay.

One February afternoon, sitting absentmindedly on a stone bench in my high school garden, I was enjoying the sun. The year's winter was nearing its end. My gaze was drawn to the ground, where I noticed a packet in a pile of peanut shells near my feet. Someone had thrown away the packet along with the shells. I picked it up out of curiosity. The packet was made out of two pages from a poetry book. It was as if a window opened inside me. I saw a universe, the same universe which had always existed but which had been invisible to me until then. It was as if the poem hidden within those two pages, which had become packaging after being sold off as waste paper, then garbage on the ground, and finally a poem again after being picked up and read by me, clicked open a lock inside me, as if I had found the key to this universe. Some poetry memory sleeping in the subconscious awakened. I felt that the words in those pages were mine, that the words asleep within had woken up. That moment marked a paradigm shift in my life. There, at that moment, poetry culminated one of its journeys and set me out on another without telling me the destination. As a poet, I am on a poem's incomplete journey.

*

My poems were first published in Delhi in a Sunday issue of the national daily *Navbharat Times* in July 1985. The poet Prayag Shukla was its Sunday magazine editor. A few weeks later, some poems appeared in a Sunday issue of another national daily based close by, *Jansatta*, where the poet Manglesh Dabral was the Sunday magazine editor. Writing and publishing poetry during that period in Delhi, I learnt to be patient with, preserve and use words, as well as to be concise. This discipline has benefited me tremendously.

*

Poetry decides its own birth. Its DNA is within us. I don't choose the words; poetry brings its own words, although we are not always able to express it perfectly. Each poem seems to be a fragment of a previous poem which was left unfinished, and which remains unfinished in every new poem. Poetry reminds us of something about the present which has happened, or the past which has yet to become the future but which cannot be remembered.

*

41

I hardly read poetry books. Initially, reading helped me understand and learn poetic syntax, but I believe that subconscious influence becomes a hindrance to developing one's own poetic style and form. However, during my travels, I do buy poetry books of regional-language poets. And I often write poems while travelling.

My poems are often inspired by nature, but many are simply based on my day-to-day activities. Driven by thoughts and feelings, my writing focuses on personal experiences. However, I don't immediately succumb to the temptation to write a poem about a given thing that has happened, because words don't come to me easily. A scene, emotion, thought, memory, word or incident registers its presence in my mind and becomes silent. I note it down in a diary, on a piece of paper or on the phone. Then, the long journey of self-study and creation begins. Thereafter, while writing a poem, that scene, emotion, thought, memory, word or incident appears again.

I don't write poems thinking about a topic in advance. Improvisation is at the core of my creative process. For example, during a visit to the Western Isles of Scotland, I saw a cormorant perched on a rock in the sea. It took a plunge into the waves and disappeared. This small image stuck in my mind. Some years later, I wrote a poem in which that cormorant's image appeared as a line towards the end. I titled the poem 'Cormorant'.

The process of creation is a puzzle, a labyrinth. As soon as my eyes open, the labyrinth is in my waking world, and as soon as they close, it automatically leaves me alone in the paraworld of the subconscious. All the elements and implements of the pain, joy, hope, depression and curiosity of language are rendered inactive. Sometimes, when turning in my sleep, I see a lot, live a lot, but I don't remember it when I wake up in the morning.

Once again, I stare at the blank paper. My gaze is drawn to the relentless rain outside. A deep ocean is sad somewhere. Has anyone ever asked this rain, 'Don't you get tired?' I run out of words.

Nothing can be said about when and where a poem begins or where it will manifest its final form. The creative process is intrinsically autonomous and unpredictable.

All I know is that I lived a long interval while writing a short poem, 'The Colour of Water'. Time, memories and past interludes, the day's many watches or colours, or some event that wanders quietly in the mental mazes – I interlace these impressions into my poems in such a way that a shape of infinity emerges in the reader's mind, and beyond it a word shape, just like an image manifests on paper after it is exposed to controlled light in a dark room. Here, in the mind, it appears in the form of a word.

पानी का रंग

यहाँ तो बारिश होती रही लगातार कई दिनों से
जैसे वह धो रही हो हमारे दाग़ों को जो छूटते ही नहीं
बस बदरंग होते जा रहे हैं क़मीज़ पर
जिसे पहनते हुए कई मौसम गुज़र चुके
जिनकी स्मृतियाँ भी मिट चुकी हैं दीवारों से

कि ना यह गरमी का मौसम
ना पतझर का ना ही यह सर्दियों का कोई दिन
कभी मैं अपने को ही पहचान कर भूल जाता हूँ

शायद कोई रंग ही ना बचे किसी सदी में इतनी बारिश के बाद
यह क़मीज़ तब पानी के रंग की होगी।

THE COLOUR OF WATER

Rain falling, day after day,
as if trying to clean off
our permanent stains,
but all it does is discolour
this well-worn shirt,
and wash the memory
of all the passing seasons
from the walls.

This is not summer
nor autumn nor winter:
sometimes I recognize myself,
then forget.

Maybe after so much rain
all colour will be washed out
and my shirt then be the colour of water.

(Translated by Lucy Rosenstein with Bernard O'Donoghue)

I do not have a remote control for writing. It's not as if the moment I start writing, all anguish and sadness will spread onto blank paper and peace will permeate within me. To know what poetry writes within me, I can't get a grip on the dialogues lost in the waves arising from writerly agitation, let alone transfer them onto paper through my hands. Nature, people, society, circumstances, feelings, desires, hopes, love, fear, rain, summer, autumn – you just need to set out, and words begin to flow by themselves. The direction of composition is not linear. And of course, not everything can be included in a single poem.

*

I believe every language has its own geography, its own dictionary. I write poems in Hindi, but in the geography of English, far away from the geography of Hindi. Somebody once asked me, 'Do you still dream in Hindi?'

For a long time, I have lived in Bath, a city in southwest England. It is lush with a variety of plants and biological species which do not exist in North India, so they do not have Hindi names. There are bird sounds, but the names associated with those sounds do not immediately come to mind. Translations can be found for them, but they are too literal to be useful in writing. Therefore, equivalent meanings and expressions have to be coined – for example, finding an equivalent for the Scottish word bog or the canopy-like pine trees growing near the Adriatic coast. The English robin looks slightly different from the Indian robin. Similarly, there are two birds which appear to be the same size, but in England the black bird is black and prefers to live alone, whereas the Indian myna is black, brown or speckled and roosts in flocks. The backyard indeed has sparrows that help bridge geographical distance and diversity. However, it is peculiar that I easily include the black bird or the robin in the poem. We had a neem tree outside the house in Delhi, but here in Bath we have a rowan tree in the backyard. Both are cherished, but the layers of my spiritual connection with them are different. One is in the present in front of me, whereas the other grows in my memory.

I believe that poetry is a process in itself. It is a statement, an expression of an active practice within and without life. Sometimes I feel I am still sitting on that same school bench… and life is happening in that poem. The poem is regulating its configuration, form, tone, sensations and images. Present in the words, it can hear, touch, see, breathe. It is alive. I'm living it.

I believe that poetry is not in the syntax of words, whether written or typed; it is within the reader. The voice present in words can speak again only when another voice reads them.

Sometimes we recognise it, and sometimes it dissipates in the noise of our inner world. To me, poetry is a dialogue between 'I' and 'you'. It is detached. It has no taste. Yet, possessed, attached, dispassionate, sweet and salty like love, as well as taste-free like a breath, its written word is only its imagination, its memory, which awakens in the mind as soon as it is read. Memories are not only for those who live life but also for those who can remember and recall. To live poetry through poetry makes this possible.

The printed words on the page we see and read are actually a translation of an experience in which a truth has been engraved. Poetry is translated into a language twice: first when it is written down and again when it is read and heard. In my poems, nestled in a quiet nook of language, I keep returning to the questions of truth, love, identity, memory, destiny, reality and nature. In other words, they are by my side like a shadow, dissatisfied with their own answers. In the midst of this bustle, I am so engrossed in the exploration of the daily internal geography of the far and the near that I can even hear my footsteps, see their shadow leaning between the words on paper. Setting a standard is not my intention behind writing. Benchmarks, I think, have already been established. They exist like the laws of nature. All that needs to be done is confirm their presence. I repeatedly return to the questions of – rather, the answers to – truth, love, fear, identity and reality. My poems record the unease inherent in the meaning and purpose of the changing conditions of life and nature as I get to know them intimately and merge with them. I do not have a template for writing.

Hour after hour, staring at the silence of the blank page in front of me, soaking under my own umbrella in my own rain as I go about my daily routine, I have searched for an uncertain address in the paths of life, and sometimes something happens all of a sudden. Surprise is the only certainty. Living in the memory of poetry, it is not possible to enclose its interior within this essay with words. The words in my own dictionary are not enough, and not meaningful enough, for me to put the final full stop in a poem. That's why, as I step from one poem to another, I wonder whether my destination is my own memory, a mirage or a fantasy. The future was once a past I no longer remember, but when I live it, my present comes alive, just as it does when I open my eyes in the morning. Shutting off my inner noise, I listen attentively to the cacophony of silence, hoping to recognise that word, the alarm that wakes us up so we can live in a dream again.

Part Two:
Making Poems

The Archaeology of Sound

Bejan Matur

Translated from the Turkish by Ayça Türkoğlu

At first, all I hear are the sounds, there are no words. It's like slipping into a whirlpool of sound, a vortex. Moving through that vortex, at some point I feel the need to stop and record my feelings, and if I've got my notebook and pen on me – which I usually have – I turn the sounds I hear into words. Perhaps I'd write a song or a symphony if I knew how to write music. What I sense at first are sounds for which there are no words, coming to me from far away, perhaps from the depths of the cosmos. It's like I can only meet with a poem when I resonate on the same level as the sheer rhythm of nature. I might describe it in simpler terms as a trance state, one I have no control over. I find it easiest to enter this kind of trance state when I'm walking in nature, or particularly when I'm visiting historical, archaeological sites. As I walk around these ancient places, which hold a kind of timeless energy, I sense voices in the stone speaking to me. I think what I'm doing in these moments is making words from the sounds that I hear.

I'm like a tape recorder, like a machine that takes a breath of air from nature and gives it back as words.

Sometimes there are moments where I get a deep sense, a strange intuition, of where, in what place, a poem is waiting for me. I feel its location in my heart, and I make my way straight towards that unborn poem. It's like responding to a summoning call. I have no control over it. And I'm rarely mistaken. No matter where I've been summoned to, I know there will be a poem waiting for me.

I sit right down and record the sounds I hear in my notebook, as a poem. If I don't have my notebook and pen with me, the rhythm I have heard will mingle with the nature around me and disappear. My feelings of gratitude grow every time I manage to catch the broken rhythm of a poem that flies away at the slightest hint of interference.

What I've described so far is the moment the inspiration for a poem comes to me. Next, I'll look at how I shape a poem and how I fit it into the structure of a whole book. Like I said, the former is a spiritual, cosmic experience, something outside of my control. The latter, on the other hand, is a disciplined process with its own internal mathematics and architectural understanding, and one over which my consciousness exerts total control. My method has not changed since I first began writing poems and I'm sticking with it.

I set aside the lines I note down in my notebook in fits of ecstasy – those intense expressions I quickly scribble down at the first sign of inspiration, when I still don't quite know what they mean – leaving them to sit for a long time. Sometimes I'll leave them for months, even years.

During this time, I never open up my notebooks and take a look inside. And I never let anyone else take a look either. I hide them away carefully. The aim of this is to allow the intensity of those feelings to cool off, to create distance between myself and those feelings. This ensures the feelings don't blur my conscious mind. I wait patiently for the time when my notebooks open of their own accord.

Once I feel I've gained enough objective distance from the poem, the editing stage begins. While I tend to sense a poem when I'm walking or on the move, when I come to edit the poem and create its final draft, I need a desk and a quiet room.

I put any travel plans aside, of course. I need to be at home and have a large chunk of time to myself. The editing stage takes months and, during that time, I work with almost a novelist's discipline.

I start by carefully reading back to myself what I've written in my notebooks. I pick the poems I find most significant and write them out by hand on sheets of paper, over and over again. I don't make any additions to the poem. Instead, I chip away at it. I work like a sculptor. I get to the essence of the poem through a process of whittling. One by one, I purge the poem of clichés and overtly emotional expressions, because I believe poetry is fundamentally the product of our sense for what is true. A poem contains within it a force that protects the truth of the poem and that's where editing meets its limits. The poem allows the poet to pare away its language up to a point but, again, it is the poem that decides where the poet must stop.

Eventually, I reach a stage where the poem will not let anything more be removed. As hard as I try, I can't go any further. I think I've always had a sense of the kind of truth and organic integrity a poem carries, of a poem as a living organism. These are the times when the poem resists me.

Once there are no words left to strip away for the sake of meaning, I move on to reading the poem aloud, to get the sound just right. I do these readings at different times of day. Sometimes I read in the early morning, sometimes I read late at night, in the hope of capturing the true feeling and rhythm of the poem. I'll sometimes find that a line I liked at night no longer reads well to me in the morning, and I'll get rid of it.

The next stage begins with writing the poems up on the computer. At this stage, I make my final cuts and do a first print-out.

Poems become more visible once they have been typed up and this gives me a clearer idea of what to cut. The integrity of the poem and its boundaries become clearer once it is on the page, and I continue cutting what I've typed up.

I actually write many more poems than I publish. I don't agree with taking up the reader's time with mediocre, clichéd poetic expressions. I'm aware that my desire for perfection and meticulousness tends to tire me out. But this is the approach I've taken since I started and it hasn't changed. When I'm preparing a poem to meet its readers, I don't grant myself any grace; instead, I turn harsh.

Some time later, another, more technical phase begins. I don't give the poems page numbers, as this lets me determine more easily where they'll sit in a book. This is how chapters come about. Sometimes a poem won't fit into any of the chapters and, ultimately, it won't make it into the book. I have files of 'surplus' poems, which I call solitary poems, poems that nobody knows about yet. I have hundreds of unpublished poems. Maybe one day I'll be able to put together a book of them. I can't decide on that at the moment. They're waiting quietly for their time to come.

Once the printed poems are almost finished, I spread them out on the floor of the room I'm working in, or on the floor of the living room, like pieces of cotton, and set about doing what feels like a kind of dressmaking. I look to see which poems have a kinship with one another, which might sit in harmony with each other. This brings the themes more clearly to the fore. I place poems with similar themes on top of each other. This ordering by theme will change a number of times, too. Sometimes a poem which was in the middle will rise to the top. Or vice versa. The poems are on the move, looking for the spot where they'll be most comfortable. After ordering them by theme, the chapters begin to take shape.

The location and order of the chapters also determines the book's meaning, its internal rhythm and flow. Like I said, I look at the pieces before me with the discipline of a novelist. I feel my way along with an architectural, mathematical intuition, to ensure each and every poem finds its rightful place. The names of the poems often come before the chapter names. I have to name most of the poems in order to be able to give the chapters themselves names.

The book's name always comes towards the very end. There have been times when I've been unable to pick a title for months.

For the final step, I give the draft of the book to a few people whose taste I trust, for them to read. It's rare, but I might remove some poems based on the feedback they give me. And sometimes, following my friends' advice, I'll leave in a poem I was thinking of cutting. In this way, the book finds its own boundaries and the poems find homes for themselves, and both become a living organism ready to meet their readers.

I currently have ten books of published poems. In my pursuit of poetry, spanning nearly thirty years, the most fundamental tendency I've noticed in myself is my passion for sensing, feeling, and writing poems, and then turning them into books. I carry out every stage with great love. There's a naturality and a flow to it. But once the poems make it into a book, my interest wanes and I'm hypnotised once again by dreams of the poems I might write. I love chasing after poems still unborn.

My poems seem different to me once they're in a book. It's as if they've separated from me and have lives of their own. I don't tend to have much interest in my published poems. Sometimes I feel like I live to serve the poems, like my mission since birth has been to be faithful to them. It's as if my duty in this life is to dig them up, unearth them from the soil, from rock, from the cosmos, like an archaeologist.

Once a book is finished, goes to press, and then reaches readers, my relationship with the poems changes dramatically. Like I said, I have a duty to pick up on poems and record them and all I want to do is respond to their call. I've felt this way for nearly thirty years. Divining poems is the only thing that interests me. I sense the truth hidden there. And my aim is to move a little closer to that truth. As I say this, I'm aware that it's not at all easy to get to the secret of a poem.

In recent years, alongside my Turkish poetry, I've started writing poems in Kurdish, my mother tongue. The reason it's taken me so long to start writing in Kurdish is undoubtedly due to Kurdish being completely banned during my childhood. We were forbidden from speaking Kurdish at school, let alone receiving our education in Kurdish.

Later, I learnt to write Kurdish under my own steam. My written Kurdish bears the local characteristics of the region where I was born. I prefer it that way. I think it's important to protect regional dialects that face the risk of total erasure. Of course, I need an editor's support to make sure what I write is understandable.

But as far as my own, personal story is concerned, beginning to write in Kurdish has had a deep, unsettling effect that I can't put into words. To make this a little easier to understand, I want to talk about my mother. My mother cannot read or write and her Turkish is poor. She can't read or understand the poems I write in Turkish. I'll never forget how her eyes sparkled with emotion when I first told her I had started writing in Kurdish. These days, my mother – who can't read or write – edits my poems in Kurdish.

My mother has become my editor and I consult her on many words and expressions. She is the person I trust most and refer to most when writing my Kurdish poems.

There's something healing and nourishing about writing in Kurdish. It's as if it is mending the hole that opened up between my mother and me, between me and my home, when I started to lose my language. I feel complete.

My Kurdish poems are definitely different from my Turkish writing. In Kurdish, I write with a greater feeling of naivety. I think I've captured a more innocent form of expression in Kurdish. It might also have something to do with the fact that Kurdish is the language of my childhood. In Kurdish, a more traditional, more organic sound comes and settles in my poetry of its own volition. It's like I capture a more feminine, more childlike sound. Of course, there's also the impact of the nature of the Kurdish language, the fact that it was banned for years, that I was cut off from it, and the painful history visited upon the Kurdish people. Last year, a selection of my Kurdish poems was published in an anthology released in the UK. I will also publish them in book form when the time comes.

And as much as I love poetry, I think I love reading poetry in my mother tongue even more.

When I read Kurdish, I feel like I'm reading a song or a lullaby. The sound is more musical, flowing from my spirit and onto my tongue. I catch hold of the familiarity of my mother tongue.

With Kurdish poetry, the emotional distance between me and the words disappears of its own accord. It's like I'm more myself. When I write in my mother tongue, it's as if I experience the healing power of language, and poetry in particular, all the more deeply.

Substantial Words: Mastering the Gabay

Asha Lul Mohamud Yusuf

Translated from the Somali by Martin Orwin

There are two ways in which poetry comes to be composed: from the imagination, or prompted by something in real life. A poem can be beautiful, or it may not be so beautiful when it is prompted by some difficult situation or bad thing that has happened in reality.

The first time I wrote a poem, I chose the gabay form[1]. The gabay is the highest form of poetic composition. It is the 'king' of poetry forms and, when someone is new to it, it is difficult for them to compose a gabay. God, though, made it easy for me. Thanks to God, I spoke in this first poem about the difficulties facing Somali women living in the diaspora. I called the poem 'Gocasho' ('Remembrance'), and shared it on some Somali-language websites. Many people reacted to it and contacted me asking if it was my first poem or if there were others I had written before. When I told them that it was my first one, they were very surprised.

After I started writing poems, I learned much about the different classical forms that poetry in my language can take, and I wrote poems in several of them, taking whichever one I felt best suited

---

1   Translator's note: The gabay is a long-line form of poetry in Somali which comprises two half-lines of unequal length, each with its own metrical pattern. Like all Somali poetry it is alliterative in that every half-line must have at least one word beginning with the same sound which runs consistently through the whole poem.

my subject matter. However, time and again, I returned to composing in the gabay form, the king of poetry.

Each time I make a poem, I try to choose substantial words, which are rooted in the traditions of the nomadic culture. When someone reads or listens to these words, they call to mind the language which was used in the past – for example to describe the utensils and vessels that women would craft by hand, used in family huts built (by women) from woven mats and grasses in the traditional way.

I include substantial words in my poems so that young people from my community benefit from them also. I take care that what I write doesn't include the language of the street or new words which young people use in their speech, because I believe that literature enriches and expands the language; it takes care of it, so that it is not lost. The people who are experts in literature say that literature is the place where the Somali language is brought down from or 'downloaded' from. I take this responsibility seriously, and so give my gabays the weight they deserve by choosing serious words of high quality. I listen to and am fuelled by the major poets such as Xasan Ganey, Maxamed Ibraahim Warsame 'Hadraawi' and many others whose poems I like very much for their content and substance.

The gabays I compose or write are many. Among them are those in which I speak about the difficulties women face; about politics; about love; and other issues in society. I always like to support women in my creative output.

If I speak of the person who creates poetry, then generally what is needed, what the poet must do, is to take care, because composing a gabay is not something to be taken lightly. One must follow the conventions of the form, its fundamental structural requirements and characteristics. It is necessary for every poet to fulfil the conditions of its construction, the alliteration, the topic and the choice of words, so that from all perspectives its art is complete and it becomes a gabay which will leave a legacy. It is right that the poet stays away from clannism, from causing conflict and from insult.

I myself try to take care, as much as I can, to follow the conditions of the gabay, its manners and behaviour so that it becomes a worthy and valuable gabay which the people will like and benefit from. Literature speaks about the thoughts of the people, and, since you wish to enter into the mind of someone else with a poem – into their feelings – you must, in all ways, construct a very beautiful work of art which will convey what you wish to say to them.

When I wish to make a gabay, or choose the seed for it or allow a gabay to come to me, I first find the topic. Then I select the alliterating sound, the letter, and then I begin the gabay. The choice of alliterating sound is very important, as it needs to carry the topic of the poem, and vice versa. Sometimes I have to change the letter a few times until I find one which is suitable.

There is some poetry in which certain sounds, for example the 'h' sound, are very beautiful, such as in love poems or poems about the environment, peace or parents (although I have still not composed a gabay about parents). I compose gabays on many different topics and the way each poem comes to me differs: for some it is through happiness, for some it is through sadness, and for others it is through a desire to relay the beauty of my country. I love to compose poetry about when the rain falls and fresh water lies on the land, about the verdure when the trees bud and flowers cover them, about the sky full of clouds and many things which I cannot sum up here, yet which fill my mind.

As I mentioned above, I first began composing poetry to support women, and it was the difficulties faced by women and girls that motivated me to write – to give examples and share the troubles they have. Although not all women face the same problems, most of them have difficulties that deserve to be spoken of.

I compose gabays about all women of the world, but especially Somali women. Most Somali women face difficulties whether they are abroad or in the Horn of Africa, so I support them with my creative vision.

The most serious problems affect young girls who are raped by men and are denied their rights. There are also young women and girls who are used for money. After the man has done what he wants to do, he leaves her on her own, pregnant and unable to tell her family, and she suffers terribly, feeling resentment and regret. Afterwards she may consider it in her interest to throw the infant away. Or she may choose to tell her family, who then beat her or cause her serious harm. I composed a poem called 'May a Girl Not Go with Him' on this subject. The poem alliterates on the hard 'g' sound. Part of the poem is given below.

Nin gadhkiyo gafuurkii cirradu gees walba u dhaafta
Oo ganbiyay diinteeniyoo dhaqankii gaylaanshay
Goobayaala fiidkoo intaa guuro bahalleeya
Curdankeennii gaagaabshay oo gaw ka wada siiyey
Oo hablaha wakhtigu gaasirana gini ku maalaaya
Galoofyada gabaanaday xayadii gabadhi yaay raacin

A man with grey hair spread throughout his beard and
    moustache
Who has turned against our religion and has kicked away
    the culture
Who stalks around at night like a wild animal
Who has cut short our children and finished them off
Who gives money to do what he wants for a short time with girls
The camel with no milk, such a man, worthless, with no
    shame, may a girl not go with him.

There are also young girls who cannot speak out, who are not able to fend for themselves and who are still living in their parents' house. Some are very young, up to ten years and some even younger, and it can happen that people of the wider family who are living in the same house molest them whenever they want. When I hear of this abuse, I weep from my heart. From this depth of feeling I composed the following part of the same poem.

Ninka gaban aan qaan gaadhin oo gurin gurcaynaysa
Oo garab carjow leeyahoo gurada aan dhaafin
Oo weli goshii hooyadeed guriga hoos joogta
Kufsi ganaca gooynaaya ee mariyay gaaleefta
Gafanaha mindida gaasirta ah geliyey ee dooxay
Waa good dhashiisii cunee gabadhi yaay raacin

The man who takes a child, a girl not yet mature, who plays
    still in front of the house
Whose shoulder is still tendon-like, who's not left the
    children's part of the hut
Who, still in the house, is by her mother's hem,
Rapes her, cuts her pancreas, brings the blunt knife to her,
That parasitic tick of a man, who stabs and pierces with the dagger:
He's a venomous serpent, snatcher of offspring, may a girl
    not go with him.

Something which is a growing trend in Somali society is the misuse of technology to control women. For example, a husband might record a video of his wife lying in bed without any clothes, without her consent. Or an unmarried man might trick a woman into sending him videos of her unclothed body parts, saying, 'I'll marry you so this will never leave my hands,' and later use the videos to blackmail the woman into doing everything he wants, by threatening to share them on social media. On this issue I composed the following section of the poem, in which I use some contemporary words:

Ninka gaaridii uu qabee gogol la jiifaysay
Ee xilaha Guule uga dhigay gaarna uga yeelay
Gurboodkiyo carruurta u dhashee guudka ugu qaaday
Go'iisiyo marada uga dhawayd gadaya ceebteeda
Misna geliya Feysbuugga ee dunida gaadhsiiya
Waa gocor xishoodkii gaboo garashadii beelay
Oo damiirka laga gawracee gabadhi yaay raacin

Ninka guurka kaa doonayee gacanta kuu haadshay
Giraan giriya haasaawahee gacalisooy baana
Gayaankaba adaan kaa xushoo gama'a ii diiday
Garka iyo wadnaha baad tihiyo gobo'da dhiiggayga
Amaan aan qalbiga gaadhahayn kugu gamsiinaaya
Misna guraya xumahaaga oo goorkastaba sheega
Yuutuub intuu galin lahaa gabadhi yaay raacin

The man who betrays the good woman he has married and
    lain with in bed,
Whose duties God gave her to do for him, who made her
    special to him,
Who bore children for him and raised them with love,
Who is closer to him than his own clothes… The man who
    sells her shame
And puts it on Facebook, exposing her to the world,
Is a useless person who lacks shame, has lost all sense,
Whose morality has been cut from him, may a girl not go with him.

The man who proposes marriage and offers his hand,
Who circles around with sweet words like 'O darling,
Of all womankind, it's you I choose and I cannot sleep
    because of it,
You are the milk vessel and the heart and the drops of my blood.'
Who showers praise on you that isn't sincere
Who collects your sordid secrets, telling you repeatedly
He would never put it on YouTube, may a girl not go with him.

In all honesty, when I recite this gabay, I feel so much pain, as if those abuses are there in front of me or as if I'm with the person they are happening to. A Somali proverb says, *Kor biliseed kabba is ma dheera*, which means that although one woman may have faced grave difficulties and others lesser ones, they all nevertheless face problems.

There are many difficulties facing women, and I hope that they disappear generally from the world and that women may live in happiness. There is the other side: if I see among women those who have achieved something, who work in high positions, who are neither angry nor resentful, who live in happiness and who have moved on from being attached to an ignorant person, I encourage them to continue on from there and not to go back. I hope that the discussion gains confidence and strengthens, and that high-achieving women strive to help their sister women who are in difficulty.

Mythology As Metaphor

Diana Anphimiadi

Translated from the Georgian by Natalia Bukia-Peters

There is nothing in the world that does not translate into the language of poetry. If you don't believe me, look at Homer's Iliad. The language of poetry can fit everything into its domain of existence, making everything poetically significant, poetically real, poetically proven.

You will hear a thousand opinions on poetry. Some people are completely indifferent to it and are interested in it in the way one might be interested in the replacement of the Minister of Culture in a minor European state. Some people cannot live without it, while for others it is something hateful, pathetic, completely incomprehensible.

Perhaps everyone is right in their own way. Poetry, although it is very tangible through voice and text, is not easy to pin down because, understandably, everyone has their own version of it.

For some, poetry is an ancient text of Sanskrit, while for others it is complex texts of Dante or Rustaveli. Someone else may prefer verses sent on WhatsApp, or the party toasts they themselves propose, marvelling at their erudition.

Language is a chemistry from which we can obtain the vitality of humans, or conversely obtain substances that are deadly. If vital and deadly words exist, then such things as poetry and literature exist too.

For me, poetry is a paradox, because it must create something as yet non-existent and non-present out of existing, real, experienced, universally acknowledged linguistic formulas. It must use oral language to create a kind of social dialect that everyone can hear but far fewer can understand.

Poetry is as much a dialectical island as, say, Fereydan among other dialects of the Georgian language – a dialect spoken by Georgians exiled to Iran approximately 300 years ago which is comprehensible as both Georgian and not-Georgian at the same time. But while Fereydan is actually still spoken by parts of the Georgian-speaking population in some villages in Iran, nobody speaks the language of the great poets Anna Kalandadze, Vazha-Pshavela, Davit Tserediani or even Rustaveli, nor have they ever spoken it. Because it is not in fact a spoken language but a linguistic reality, a heightened space of sacral ritual, old or new inscriptions. Therefore, when we tell our primary school pupils, or foreigners who are interested in learning the Georgian language, that we read and write Georgian as we speak it (because it has a phonetic script), when it comes to poetry this turns out not to be correct.

*

In the beginning, I tried to understand the process of creating poetry, the birth of a metaphor etc, by observing myself in the act of writing.

When I became a master's student in the Department of General and Applied Linguistics at Tbilisi State University, I came up with an ambitious and perhaps brazen idea: to linguistically analyse the intention behind a text as it was being created, and forensically compare that to an external reader's perception of the finished text. I wanted to act as an author-scientist, to formulate my own theory, and to have empirical material as well, and in this way to describe what path the poetic sign takes between formation and perception. In short, I wanted to discover whether there is some kind of universality, a rule, a law of transformation according to which the poem I wrote becomes the one you, the reader, will read.

In the process of writing a poem for this experiment, I carefully annotated a metaphor according to the ideas I meant by/within it. I broke down the metaphor into semiotic signs and marked them up. Then I prepared a linguistic questionnaire in which I asked readers, that is, the participants of the experiment, to describe how they understood the metaphor in the finished poem.

It turned out that my experiment was doomed to failure from the start, because it is impossible to describe the process of creating text; you can't reduce it to formulas. And of course there are no two people in the universe who perceive the same metaphor or poetic event in the same way.

*

Why did I start with such an extended introduction?

I probably had the wrong plan from the beginning, because the majesty of poetry is precisely in the multiple understandings and interpretations of one linguistic sign.

I would like to mention here that the language I write in, Georgian, gives especially many opportunities for such multiples because of its unique properties: for example our verb declensions can contain subjects, direct and indirect objects and even directionality within a single word; while the absence of grammatical gender enables our love poems to be about whatever kind of couple a reader wishes to see.

One area known for being rich in interpretative potential is mythological archetypes. Myth and poetry have a lot in common.

First of all, just as in ancient myth every tree and spring has its own God, so words of all kinds have their unique power. If you tell a chicken – shoo – it runs away, if you tell a cat – psst – it immediately disappears. Words have power, and this power is deployed especially within the space of a poem.

If poetry is a game, then playing with archetypes makes it a more complex and interesting game. Carl Jung writes that no matter how paradoxical it may be, every generation knows more about mythological symbols than the people of the previous generation, because of the layers of interpretation and meaning-making that have accumulated on the symbols over time. Because of this, mythological heroes and heroines are incredibly rich material, and are a very useful resource to the poet.

*

My 2009 poetry collection *Notes on Mythology* reimagines several characters from Greek mythology. 'Notes on Mythology' is actually the name of the first poem I wrote for the book, though I hadn't planned on writing a whole book on this topic at the time. The poem, a kind of conjecture to understand the famed mythical fables in a new way, simultaneously opened up the world of the living, Olympus and Hades. It was followed by other poems; first there were stories of gods, then semi-gods, and then men.

As it progressed, *Notes on Mythology* became a conceptual collection, a unity of separate poems, a single story – my personal mythology. It was written in exactly one year, and even the order of the poems is important for understanding the book.

For example, my second poem relates to new information I found out about my own identity. I am originally Greek, raised in the Georgian-speaking world, linguistically Georgian. I never thought about what I had to do with the Hellenic world besides the Greek-sounding ending of my surname. But it turned out that genetics and, if you like, 'ancestral memory', plays a very big role.

Lately, I have observed that once a nation begins to wander, that is, as a result of forced or voluntary migration, it continues to be migrant. For example, the Pontic Greeks, of whom I am a representative, to this day, despite returning to this historic homeland, still cannot find their place. In modern Greek poetry – especially in the Pontic Greeks' poetry who newly arrived from here – the myth of the perpetually wandering Odysseus is particularly resonant. This theme can also be found in many of my poems; knowing about my heritage makes me see myself and this spiritual journey in a new way.

The second poem in my collection was about the Odyssey, but the main character of the story became not Odysseus but Penelope. In the poem, Odysseus has not gone anywhere, he has remained at home, but Penelope thinks he is far away – she wants him to be far away and to miss him from far away.

And so it went on. It turned out that I was interested most of all in women. Although the ancient Greek Pantheon is patriarchal in its essence, led by Zeus, who is adorned with all the qualities of the man of the patriarchal world, women are especially interesting to me. Not just women with special, divine ability, but also ordinary mortal women. They are, in various myths or legends, mainly objects rather than subjects, their fates decided by others, but in fact they deserve to be at the centre of the story.

*

In the end, these were the poems included in the collection:

To my father
Exercise
Sameness
Rules for pedestrians
Nymph
Cosmogony
Mermaid Lullaby
Ritual Chronicles
Mythology
Prayer for those who died
Dwarves
Eurydice
Danae
Ariadne
Acteon
Antigonus
About the Centaur
Galathea
Ganymede
Hero and Leander
Helen
Curse - Circe
Cassandra
Pandora
Cassiopea
Ithaka
Medea
The Simple Truth About The Golden Fleece
Clytemnestra
Iphigenia
Nausicaa
Consequences of global warming

The book turned into a kind of classical drama, but one where all the actions are carried out by the reader. The stories of the mythological heroines are my story, and also the story of all readers. I was interested in the idea of creating characters who are unchanged from their mythological roots but placed in a different time and space, in different environmental conditions and context.

'Iphigenia' is about all violently married women. In many countries of the world, including Georgia, underage marriage is still practised. 'Clytemnestra' is about a character who can no longer adapt to the person who returned home in his slippers and pyjamas. In another poem, Pandora, who expresses emotions in the form of words, is a poet. 'Cassiopeia' is the story of every woman who was punished for perceiving her own strength and opportunity in reality. Nausicaa is a girl who enjoyed promiscuous trysts, and who was pushed into contrived conflicts. Helen is the main character in the most important drama of humanity, but she herself is always forgotten. Antigonus is the modern world that has become an area of right-wing and leftist struggle, while Medea is every woman who wants to escape a constraining world.

All of these characters are metaphors – they are myself and the reader at the same time. I used them to tell the stories of modern, 21st-century women in a way that shows how unchanged the archetypes are, how the patriarchal world tries to subjugate women, and yet women still manage to become goddesses.

In fact, the most important metaphor is that all people carry an archetypal experience, we are simultaneously demiurge and ruling gods, goddesses, immortal heroes of war, travellers in fatal adventures, deceived and vengeful women, people who turn to nature to protect themselves.

Mircea Eliade wrote about myth in his most important work:

'Because myth portrays the heroic deeds of supernatural beings and their sacral strength, it serves as a model of all the most important human behaviours.'

I continued to create mythical characters in my subsequent books; that is to say, to keep on working on the puzzle of myself. It was neither an obsession nor my own sense of purpose; it was kind of a game, the story of every woman through my brain, heart, body, and most importantly, words.

მედუზა–გორგონა

როცა გითხარი, არაფერი ხდება-მეთქი,
უბრალოდ მოგატყუე.
ხდება, ყოველდღე ხდება
ხიდები,ხედები...
რადგან სიყვარულს დავმორჩილდი,
დავდივარ, ვისთვის – თავმოქრილი,
ვისთვის კი – სარკე – შეხედვისას
ქვავდები,
ხევდები.
როცა გითხარი, არაფერი ხდება – მეთქი,
უბრალოდ დამავიწყდა. იმ დღიდან
ყველა ცხენოსანი, ანდა ქვეითი
ჩემს სახელს,
(სახელს თავმოქრილის)
ატარებს ფარად...
თუ ქვას მესვრიან
იბრუნებენ პასუხს ქვებითვე...
რომ გითხარი, არაფერი ხდება – მეთქი,
    უბრალოდ მოგატყუე,
არაფერიც კი აღარ ხდება, ვსუნთქავ, ვარსებობ,
გული – მხუთავი სიმსივნეა მკერდში, ძუძუსთან,
მელოდიები ამოვქერი, მუსიკის ავი თვისებები,
    მეტასტაზები,
რომელთაც მოაქვთ დაკარგული დღეების ხმები
გული – ქრისტესისხლას ბუჩქია,
ხმება.
ეჰ, ღირდეს მაინც – ღამით კისერს ჰკიდია
    ბეწვით
თავი – დილით კი მორჩენილი ჭრილობა მეწვის,
მერე, თავიდან...

Diana Anphimiadi

MEDUSA

When I said nothing happened
I lied to you.
It happens, it happens every day,
on bridges, in open spaces.
Because I yielded to love
I walk, for some an object of shame,
for others a mirror. Whoever looks at me
is turned to stone,
frozen.

When I said nothing happened
I simply forgot. Since that day
all the riders, all the pedestrians
have carried my name
(*Shame*) as a shield.
If a stone is thrown at me
I answer with stone…

When I said nothing happened,
I just lied.
This is what happens: I breathe, I exist.
My heart is a choking tumour, near the breast.
I cut out the tunes,
the malignant music, metastasis
which brings back the voices of lost days.
My heart is a celandine,
parched.
My love, can it be worth it? At night
my head hangs from my neck by a single hair
then morning, and the pain of the healed wound
and it starts all over again…

Translated by Natalia Bukia-Peters with Jean Sprackland

Take the Poem-Shaped Bits Out of the Poems

Yu Yoyo

Translated from the Chinese by Dave Haysom

What is it, I sometimes wonder, the magic of poetry that we receive and relay, in the west and in the east, in Greece and in China, across millennia of history? To my mind it is not only the spiritual element, the encounter with the sublime; the emergence and perpetuation of poetry must be understood as being bound up in and being of the reality of life, birth, existence.

The majority of the works in *The Book of Songs*, China's earliest collection of poetry, deal with the joys and hardships of ordinary people, transformed into ballads to be passed on orally. There are a couple of minority languages in China that, to me, seem like an externalisation of poetry: Tibetan, and Yi. I am told, for example, that when Tibetans want to settle disputes, they wield poems as arguments. These two languages are spoken in a way that corresponds perfectly with poetry; the addition of line breaks would perhaps make poems of their conversation. There is something miraculous about a form of language that so naturally forms poems, and surely occupies the position closest to poetry.

Writing in Mandarin Chinese, I am also trying to create something resembling a naturally formed poem, but the word *natural* is the antithesis of *fashioned*, just as there are some innate talents that cannot be acquired. But actual writing must be fashioned. To constitute a form of artistic expression, modern poetry must be interwoven with human creativity. So how can the two halves of this antithesis be brought together?

By bringing *fashioned* as close as possible to *natural*.

Natural can mean two different things when referring to a poem, according to my understanding of the concept. The first is in the sense of 'necessary', i.e. the poem appears in the only form that will allow for its complete expression . The second is in the sense of 'unadorned', i.e. the poem appears in 'plain' language, without any ornamentation. These considerations bring us to the craft of poetry, and the question of poetic technique.

Of poetic technique there is much to discuss. The stylistic devices of ancient times serve the same function as modern poetry's non-sequiturs, antitheses, and shifts across different levels of reality: they achieve a defamiliarising effect. But this angle of approach pushes poetry towards a more rule-bound, mechanistic kind of manufacture, whereas poets prefer to preserve the mission of poetry – along with the *mystery* of poetry. The ineffable nature of this mystery could easily be interpreted as elitist hauteur. And poetry has indeed been criticised for this very reason. The mysterious always elicits our curiosity, complicating our feelings for a poem, sending ripples back and forth between poet and reader.

Much of what we perceive as *natural* is determined through the process of reading. Reading can feel like divine solicitude, when a poet seems to have been inspired with words from the gods. Or like a descent into the terrestrial, into nature, a synthesis of existence and feeling that is inextricable from our lives. Poems like this are usually spiritual, pure, refined; they invariably demonstrate such sophisticated command of technique that technique becomes imperceptible, and they approach an essence of language that seems to have emerged from nature, as transparent as crystal.

Yet to assert that poetry ultimately inclines towards the *untechnical* is to miss the point. Many will stand up to reject such a reductive assertion, especially the more poetically adventurous. But what I mean by untechnical is actually a kind of technique, and it shares the goal of many who are striving to optimise technique: to find some way to break out from the mass of familiar writing, from the mass of clichéd expressions, to transcend and take a step forward from the existing aesthetic dimension. I emphasise untechnical technique because the conspicuous residue of technique, together with profound concepts and exquisite stylistic devices, has created a decaying wall that guards poetry but also contains it. Vanishing this wall away is the only way to find the freedom that makes poetry viable, that makes creativity possible.

So, *untechnical*, for me, does not oppose technique; it means a different kind of technique. It means taking the poem-shaped bits out of the poems. Not writing poetry for poetry's sake. A poem is the poem it is, and any attempt to force technique upon it should be resisted. What this ultimately points towards in a new kind of aesthetic.

Since I am describing an individual perspective, I will use a short poem of my own as an example.

《哎》

ai

睡不着的时候
就把眼睛摘下来
关进小盒子里
天这么黑这么黑
连鼻孔和耳朵里面
都需要点灯

when you can't sleep
pluck out your eye
box it away
it's so very dark
even nostrils and ears
need illumination

This poem has only six lines; individually, none of them seem particularly poetic or special. None of them employ any kind of stylistic device. Anyone might have uttered them. But once these lines are combined, a certain mood becomes palpable. Not a mood that I set out to write, but one that is absorbed into the movement through space – space that saturates sight; that becomes one with the dark, the seamless, all-encompassing dark; that exists, hidden, in nuance.

It seems as though only the elimination of darkness can eliminate this discomforting mood. How can darkness be eliminated? By turning on a lamp and making everything bright. But light cannot fill the space it illuminates, and is not enough to eliminate darkness. Because true darkness comes through the sensory organs of the body, and what we really desire to eliminate is the physical discomfort of insomnia. It is our bodies that actually require illumination and comfort. Hence the idea of lighting the nostrils and ears. Why these two organs, in particular? Because they are two parts of the body that we often overlook. Light up the darkness in the corners of our body, and a kind of energy erupts, subtle yet condensed.

But turning on a light in the ears and nostrils feels too surreal. In order to make it less overt, to avoid imposing a particular poetic shape, I left things blurred. Does the light get switched on, or not? The poem does not supply an answer. This softens the point of the entire poem, and makes it seem like it signifies something and nothing at the same time. Nothing is certain, which leaves space for contemplation.

Yet the mood has already been communicated, and a common experience has been summoned: a memory of being unable to sleep, eliciting corresponding feelings that may clarify the blur of the poem. At the same time, we seem to be situated in a scene that is perfectly clear: the speaker of the poem, mired in insomnia one night, is surrounded by darkness, and can see nothing.

And so the natural texture that I pursue in poetry is ultimately realised in a state of ignorance. The process of applying technique and erasing all traces of technique, restoring nature and honesty, filtering out superfluous impurities, distilling the essence of the poem – to follow through on all this is to remove everything 'explainable' about the poem, and thus strengthen everything that is unique about the text itself. The poem is the poem itself, and everything beyond the poem is null.

A Wave Collapses
On Another Wave

Al-Saddiq Al-Raddi

Translated from the Arabic by Atef Alshaer

'Who showed you the path of the poets?' This question remains etched in my mind and memory. It is a line I read a long time ago, in a poem by the Spanish poet and playwright Federico García Lorca (1898–1936), in a selection of his poetry translated into Arabic. Lorca is one of the poets whom I most admire. His short life, full of creativity and innovation, fascinates me, especially his play *Blood Wedding* and his music. In pondering the question, I have been trying to delve deep into my memory to trace the origins of the thread that guided me to poetry and linked me to it for the first time; or the spark of lightning that uncovered me to poetry one distant night. Poetry found its way to me while I was hidden in the cave of my own secret, and I have remained its prisoner for over 30 years. Of course, that thread cannot be found, or that spark that perhaps showed me the path of the poets, without returning to the first well: childhood.

Childhood is a room of many mirrors, where the phantasms of one's first development are overlaid with snatches of early dreams, private myths, which find their way into memory and grow over time. Such myths are spoken by the mother or grandmother, accompanied by melodies and whispers of as yet unknown words. Sounds intermixed with smells. Childhood is the storehouse of the poet's myth, his own personal myths. Myths are the storehouse of his secrets, to which he always returns, as he advances on his own journey. My childhood was linked to my birthplace in the city of Omdurmán. This is the place where the Blue Nile joins with the White Nile to form the Nile River, the mighty channel which passes through the old Nubian Kingdoms of Sudan (Kush) with their illustrious history on its way up to the Mediterranean Sea. This confluence of waters is where I grew up, where my emotions and knowledge took shape, and where I received my education at every stage.

Between 1985 and 1986, when I was in my late teens, I wrote and published hundreds of poems in newspapers and journals. These were published inside Sudan, as well as in Arab cities in other countries. I also took part in forums and gatherings for poetry. These were held weekly in the three main districts of the capital, namely Omdurmán, Khartoum and Khartoum Bahri. I took part in public readings of poetry, including in cultural clubs in different areas of the city, and places such as universities and institutes of higher education. I also obtained during this period, and particularly in 1986, membership of the Sudanese Writers' Union. This allowed me to participate in weekly regular meetings with select audiences. It also opened the door for me to participate in activities in other cities beyond Khartoum.

During this time I began to receive advice on how to be a poet from everyone around me. At all times, and as happens with every poet in his beginnings, the first common advice is to read and pay attention to language and its recitation. This is important advice, one which the poet cannot do without. It was very important for me to read written poetry in Arabic. It is poetry with deep historical roots, whose schools and old and new traditions should be known. One should also know those who contributed to its development and study their work as well as the social, cultural and political environment that gave rise to it. And of course, one must survey the modern map of poetry and its icons. The modern as far as it relates to the written poetry in Arabic covers a wide map that includes countries from the Arab Morocco in Africa to the Gulf, to the Arabian Peninsula, and the Levant. The richness lies in the variety and diversity of culture. This richness feeds the written poetry of our language and enriches its currents.

But the reading and recitation of language is not enough. With talent and instinctual readiness, music was for me an important source of poetic inspiration. I come from a social and cultural environment rich and diverse in its musical traditions. It celebrates tunes from all rituals and details of daily life. These are connected to all its seasons and happy and sad occasions. My practice of music since a young age through playing melodious instruments and some percussion instruments has had an influence on the development of my poetic sensibility. I don't think a poet necessarily needs to practise the art of theatre and its traditions. But he needs to know its history and be able to have a taste for it, in order to open new horizons for the development of poetic images without limits. This gives him a philosophical depth to enrich his composition and develop his tools of expression in writing. I noticed this when I became close to friends who studied theatre and music at the Youth and Children Theatre in the city of Omdurmán.

Contemporaneous with this, my relationship with students of the faculty of Fine and Applied Arts in Khartoum contributed to my knowledge of visual arts, and their history. I also gained knowledge of modern and contemporary schools and read the history of these schools and their philosophical convictions. All of this has had a great influence on the development of my own poetic voice and my poetic experience.

*

Then came the moment to put together my first poetry collection. The importance of the first book cannot be underestimated; it can determine a poet's path in the future. The task was to sift through and choose some texts while excluding others, leaving the excluded texts to their own fate in the archives of newspapers and journals, or in the memory of their first readers. The first book is the first adventure of the poet on this long road of self-curation, which has never been smoothly paved. It begins with the selection of texts, then goes through to the editing, the choice of the book title, the manner of acknowledgment and, of course, the choice of the publisher. All these preferences and small details are very important. They may decide the way in which readers get to know you, and other poets and critics, etc. Such details and preferences indicate the place where you want your name to be, the place where you wish to go further into the journey of poetry and into your next adventures.

The moment I sat down to select the poems for my first poetry collection, I experienced a great deal of confusion. This was due to the large quantity of poems, the diversity of their subjects, and the different styles involved. The method I suggested to myself was to exclude poems where I show influence by other poetic voices. This particularly pertains to powerful and influential poets, the icons – those whom I read intensively and who formed my taste and mood in writing. They include the Sudanese poet Muhammed Al-Mahdi Al-Majdhub (1919–1982), Mohammed Abdul-Hayy (1944–1989), the Egyptian poet Amal Dunqul (1940–1983), the Palestinian poet Mahmoud Darwish (1941–2008), and the Iraqi poet Saadi Youssef (1934–2021). Their voices formed the influential poetic currents for the young poets in my own generation. In the second stage, I started to exclude poems whose content I found to be influenced by political and social issues in a direct manner. They were essentially the outcome of events I experienced during that period, and I did not find depth in their content or merit in their artistic quality. I resolved in the end to choose ten poems only. This constituted my first poetry collection, which was published under the title *Songs of Solitude*.

*

Reading in front of an audience in closed or open spaces has a particular influence on the relationship of the poet to his poem. It gives him the chance to know the poem once again, away from the paper. He comes to know its features while being carried through the air from his own voice with its different registers. The interaction of the audience with the poem gives it a new dimension. The poem does not drop itself all at once on the paper or in front of the audience. It has an ability to live its own life more than one time after it has been written. In fact, it can live even more after the death of its poet in his physical existence per se.

The poet remains constantly an amateur poet. For the writing of any poem by any poet, whatever his experience, constitutes essentially a new beginning. Creativity in poetry is a continuous process of learning, a process of destruction and construction. The writing of a new poem is ultimately the end of an amateur poet. Soon he will experience new beginnings that collapse in the wake of every progress. A wave collapses on another wave to surge forward!

Nightmare Inspiration

Yang Lian

Translated from the Chinese by Brian Holton

The source of contemporary Chinese poetry, in two words, is *nightmare inspiration*.

Nightmares: the Cultural Revolution, the Anti-Spiritual Pollution campaign, the Tiananmen massacre, exile, world-wide commercialisation, turning back history in Hong Kong, the Covid-19 pandemic, the Chained Woman, the Taiwan crisis, the White Paper movement… Nightmare, the normality of our existence.

Inspirations: the title of my first poem was 'Confession – For a Ruin'. Next, 'Earth' was based on my experience of the Cultural Revolution; *The Ritualisation of the Soul* was steeped in historical reflections on the 1980s; my 1994 collection *Yi* summed up my thoughts on China's predicament and China's language; *Non-Person Singular* was a response to the Tiananmen massacre; *Where The Sea Stands Still* was inspired by exile overseas; *Concentric Circles* connected with synchronic trends in and beyond China; *Narrative Poem* revealed one person's internal depths in a greater history; my poem 'A Tower Built Downwards' concludes with the line: 'to inwardly endure an unendurable world'. And so on: the examples here are just a small sample of my writing.

In 1980, when I travelled to the Loess plateau of western China for the first time, I filled a notebook with hundreds of poems. When I got back to Beijing, I wondered as I read them, are these poems all different? Or had I simply repeated the same poem under different titles? What is the reason for bringing a poem into being? I deleted everything except the poem cycles *Banpo* and *Dunhuang*. The former explored the *predicament of existence* and the latter the *predicament of mind*; with the addition of the *Norlang* cycle, these became my first collection in Chinese, *The Ritualisation Of The Soul* (1985).

After the Tiananmen massacre in 1989, there was shock and there were tears all over the world, but my poem '1989' ended with the line 'this is no doubt a perfectly ordinary year'. What I wanted to say was, while we were shocked by the massacre, what about the countless dead from before this time? If they were forgotten, who could guarantee that today's tears wouldn't wash memory away, in preparation for the shock of the next massacre? 1989 was certainly not a mere 'incident': it pointed out our basic predicament. From reality to history and from China to the world, how many disasters have followed hard on the heels of that year? 9/11, the Iraq War, Hong Kong, the pandemic, right up to the Ukraine War today… 'a perfectly ordinary year' – oh, when did we ever leave here?

Life is deeply permeated by politics, and if poetry writes about that, then its one and only power comes from the poet's self-interrogation.

My latest collection in English translation *A Tower Built Downwards* is a new work, but looking closer, what is *new* about it? In 2019, Hong Kong's youth took to the streets to oppose the tyrannical National Security Law, and as umbrellas like multi-coloured mushrooms were swept away by frenzied fire hoses, did people remember the bloody clothes in front of Tiananmen exactly thirty years ago? The phrase in my *Poems on Turning Back History*, 'a foundling of time' is a sigh or regret for every destroyed youth. That same year, the pandemic exploded out of Wuhan, and the numberless dead, all cherishing a vain hope of striving for meaning in their future lives, vanished into utter nothingness as they let go of this mortal realm. My poem 'For

The One Beside Me Who Vanishes' not only interrogates death, but also has a meaning in the life of the imagination:

> home is a rough sketch   a person is a rough sketch
> > howling darkness
>
> nothing can cry back

Is this illusion still deceiving us?

Every *now* is an entrance to the archaeology of a human life. Endless historical depths come from digging into it. It allows us to break through our own diachrony at every point, to arrive at the synchronic human predicament. This pierces through the surface of language to provide a poetic *grammar*, an underlying method of poetic thinking, to become aware of the dilemma, refine thought, stimulate creativity, and within an ever-deepening oeuvre, intersect with dynamic spiritual traditions.

Nightmare Inspiration is not a slogan, for it runs through the thinking and writing of *all poetry*. Because it is there, we can even, via translation, read and understand Qu Yuan, Ovid, Du Fu, or Dante, right up to contemporary poets and, in accordance with a poet's concepts of our poetry, forms and language, institute a breakthrough in comprehension to judge whether a particular poet is good, or important.[1] Novelty in form is not novelty for its own sake, but novelty because it is impossible not to innovate, for form is not otherwise enough to express profound thinking. The *importance* of poetry is that it is the only embodiment of a profundity of thought verified by quality of language.

Here the poet's self-interrogation is still the crux of the matter. On the one hand, my poem 'Researching Evil' laments the reek of blood from the Ukraine War which is saturating Europe, and at the same time, it heaves a mother's sigh for China's Chained

---

1   T.S. Eliot, *Tradition and the Individual Talent* (1919).

Woman[2]. While superficially these are thousands of miles apart, what difference does geography make to hardship? All human tragedy is rooted in the darkness of human nature. So which of us should not shoulder the responsibility for such misfortunes? In today's selfish, cynical world, where profit is running rampant – time has buried time, and ruins have covered ruins – the nightmares come flooding in, to the point that we are left unable to remember anything at all, and each of us is now our own 'one beside me who vanishes'.

Can poetry finish writing its interrogation of human nature? Should poetry finish writing this interrogation? The answer is simple – I ask, therefore I am.

2   The Chained Woman was a girl who had been trafficked and sold to a village in Jiangsu Province: after multiple rapes, she bore eight children. To stop her running away and reporting the wrong done to her, a chain was locked around her neck, and her tongue cut out: by the time she was discovered in January 2022, she was no longer in her right mind.

倒退的历史诗——致香港

一

海浪擦得雪亮　媲美头盔　盾牌
海湾像一座躺倒的大厦　塌进
黑暗中一起一伏　霓虹的对岸
轻飘飘荡漾　海市蜃楼怀抱我们荡漾
一只海鸥染红了羽毛浮游而过
一百万面玻璃幕墙擦得雪亮　倒映出历史

四

又一次　大海古老的眼泪凸透镜
哭着我们的哭　认命的人　认出
风雨象声词　复述一种劈劈啪啪的毁灭
心　早晨醒来就抵在墙上死了又死
原地挣扎的黑暗　精雕细刻到极致
奔逃和追逐是同一个姿势

八

一个时间的弃儿
分不清自己是水或玻璃
冷冷扫射的光　传递着空白的固体
依山而建的墓园里我的墓碑湿漉漉的
我的名字湿漉漉的　正活生生爬上
冷漠荒凉的绝对高度

十二

玻璃墓碑在海浪间闪耀　毁灭押送它
又一个末日走失了　提前忘记它
泡沫自我渗入泡沫他人　无痛抹掉它
诗　一艘生锈的渡轮　尽情编造它
烂出的尸骸跨着正步　总不缺周年欢呼它
一页大海的遗嘱在身边翻滚　永远没人读它

Yang Lian

POEMS ON TURNING BACK HISTORY (*for Hong Kong*)

1

ocean waves polished snow-bright   matching helmets   shields
gulf like a laid-down high-rise   collapses into
the dark rising and falling   a neon other shore
lightly rippling   the mirage embraces us and our rippling
one incarnadine-feathered seagull bobs by
one million glass curtain walls polished snow-bright   reflect history

4

once again   the convex lens of the ocean's ancient teardrop
weeps our tears   those resigned to their fate   recognise
storm's onomatopoeia   retelling the pitter-patter of ruin
hearts   wake at morning to die and die again pushing at walls
dark that motionless struggles   carefully sculpted to its limits
flight and pursuit are the same gesture

8

a foundling of time
unsure if it's water or glass
coldly shoots light   delivers blank solids
in the hillside graveyard my headstone is damp
my name is damp   alive and climbing to
indifferent desolate absolute heights

12

glass gravestone gleaming among ocean waves   ruin escorts it
one more dying day gone missing   beforehand forgets it
the foamy self seeps into foamy others   painlessly erases it
poetry   a rusty ferry boat   to its heart's content invents it
rotted-out corpses goosestep   never lacking an anniversary to
    cheer it
ocean's one-page will and testament rolls alongside   never
    anyone reading it

Translated by Brian Holton

89

Part Three:
On Language

Living in Translation *(excerpt)*

Laura Wittner

Translated from the Spanish by Will Howard

This piece is an excerpt from Laura Wittner's 2021 book, Se vive y se traduce, *an autobiographical essay on translation published by Editorial Entropía, for which Wittner was awarded a National Prize in 2023.*

To translate is to always be on someone's heels.

***

This orange ink trying to consolidate itself through the remains of green ink (as in the Claire-Louise Bennett story) resembles the transition between two translations. A voice trying to take hold, gently displacing and dispersing the previous one.

***

Someone posts a translated poem on Facebook and out come the armchair editors: they don't like that word; they don't agree with the use of inclusive language; actually, x could be y.

Someone publishes a poorly translated book of poetry. Two adjectives and an adverb before a noun, music pushed aside, lines that grow longer until they need a bracket to move them to the right. No one notices anything off, they love it, they post it on social media, they say, I adore this poet.

***

On rainy Sundays, I sometimes translate loose lines of poetry, and because they're loose, I take lots of liberties, and because I take lots of liberties, I steal them.

***

Because I'm generally not allowed to use the pronoun vos, I translate entire novels avoiding the decision between vos and tú. I consider it to be the only sport at which I excel.

***

When I'm finishing a translation of a novel and re-read the first pages I translated, I find in them the naïve and tentative style typical of the conversations we have with someone we're getting to know and who will become a great love, someone with whom we will create an intimate and shared language.

***

Does the author feel something from a distance, in her body, while I translate her text? Like a voodoo doll?

***

Damn it: 'strength' and 'effortless' in the same sentence. Damn it: 'to use' and 'to wear' in the same sentence.

***

I went to a new eye doctor, began to explain to him the struggle with translation/short-sightedness/long-sightedness, and he said to me: 'Oh, translators have it hard because…' and he perfectly described the display of planes and distances. He even talked about when we used a thousand dictionaries, before the advent of the internet. *Is this love that I'm feeling?*

Luciana: 'No, that's *never ever* going to happen. How do you say *never ever* in Spanish?'

Me: '¿Nunca jamás?'

Luciana: 'No, nunca unca.'

***

It's the final scene of the book I've been translating for months, and the narrator turns on the car radio, and I play the same song to translate these last lines because who am I without my rituals.

***

I would put together a book, or rather a chapbook, containing only the Google searches from when I'm translating, exactly the way I phrase them. But I don't know if I'm ready for something so embarrassing.

***

Only on revising the translation do I realize a certain comment had been a joke. Sometimes I become too serious while translating. The risk of misinterpretation makes me tense.

***

To translate is to wonder several times a day: 'Is that how you say it, or am I making it up?'

***

To translate is to denature and renature (and denature again).

***

Page 23, finally the semicolon appears. Gotcha! I was waiting for you. From now on, I decide I can use it if I need to, no matter how little the original uses it.

Everyone has their own rules. Every translator their own little book.

Moreover: well done, Cynan. Who would want to miss out on a punctuation mark as elegant and polyvalent as the semicolon?

***

One of the multiple points of eternal return: whether to use the 'personal a' if the direct object is not a person but an animal. Yes, no, here yes, not here, and sometimes I need to switch it up when referring to the same animal if the circumstance changes. Even with the same verb. In Cynan Jones' *The Dig*, the question is omnipresent because there are more animal characters than human ones, and the 'humanity' of these animals seems to vary depending on who is interacting with them and how.

There is no end to the meticulous work intrinsic to translation.

***

What a word, '*estiércol*', as in 'manure'. With that accent above the diphthong, that 'l' at the end, that English air, as in, 'Máicol', that suggestion of brand or portmanteau. And yet, not so: it comes from *stercus, -oris*.

Yes, I translate like this. Sometimes. Most of the time. Stopping every couple of yards to take in the scenery.

***

I'm translating Leanne Shapton. It's been a bad day. Last night, my fibromyalgia overcame me unexpectedly, after a lovely day.

I've been sitting in front of the monitor for two hours, and the words won't click into place. 'The tall pines, silhouetted against the navy sky…'

Silhouetted… I see the image, think of how many times I've translated this verb that, in Spanish, only corresponds (in sound) to a noun, *silueta*. I know it's a straightforward translation, that it can be found in my mind, not in the dictionary. But my mind won't respond, and my body hurts. My mental faculties are stalled. So I search through dictionaries, and the mouse begins to hurt my hand.

Then my daughter, who's missing school, walks in. Without saying a thing (so as not to interrupt me), she takes the scissors from a drawer in my desk. Her back is turned to me, but I hear her cut out a piece of paper.

'*Recortados*,' my mind murmurs, a tired response.

Ah, of course, that's it.

'*Los pinos altos, recortados contra el cielo azul marino…*'

***

Two months ago, I went to the Hampstead Heath Ponds in London for the first time. Juan had translated the stunning *Pondlife* by Al Alvarez, which takes place there, such that the visit had a profound relationship to the task of translation. Juan visited Al and brought him a copy of the Spanish edition. We went to swim in the ponds three times, he in the men's pond, I in the women's. We didn't go to the mixed one.

Of course I'd read Juan's version, *En el estanque*, and I'd also closely followed the translation process, so I already felt Hampstead Heath was partially mine before going there.

The place seemed magical to me when I went, and since then it hasn't stopped revealing its magic: I've already seen it mentioned in at least four books I've read or flipped through. But today it appears in the book I'm translating by Leanne Shapton. 'I wend my way up the overgrown front path.' I see Leanne walking the lush path I myself have gone down several times, which is how I understand what she means by 'overgrown', and the translation flows smoothly for the whole chapter: the ponds, the paths, the slopes, the runners, I saw it all, heard it. I smelled all of it. And I return to the idea that this is how we should translate: by coming to the place. Smelling, eating, walking.

'Puedo ver mi aliento mientras subo por el sendero selvático.'

***

And looking at it, let's say, the other way around: I've never been to Baltimore but feel as if I have because the first novel I translated, *A Patchwork* by Anne Tyler, takes place there. Nor have I been to Montreal, though I have a soft spot for it because it's where *Beautiful Losers* takes place – if it can be said to 'take place' – that wild ride of a novel by Leonard Cohen for whose translation I needed friends and friends of friends to go to certain Quebecois street corners and send me photos.

***

What's this impulse that sometimes takes hold of me to translate as I read the sentence, without letting my eyes nor my understanding move even two words ahead? *It's only rock'n'roll – but I like it.*

***

Leanne Shapton is visiting London and goes to swim in the women's pond at Hampstead Heath only once. As soon as she enters the water, she feels a shock of cold that makes her gasp, like I did.

She observes how the other women interact. She doesn't know what the right way to behave in the changing room is and imitates the others, as I did. I can't explain why I'm so moved by this shared experience. Perhaps it's because the dynamic of that changing room under the sky, of that stripping down outdoors, continually returns to my body and mind. Perhaps it also has something to do with the recent death of Al Alvarez, two months after we swam in his ponds and walked his paths with their shade and foxes.

When Juan writes to tell me Al Alvarez has died, I perceive a much deeper hurt in his message.

To translate is to inhabit another person. It is to make space inside ourselves so that they, too, may inhabit us.

***

Suzanne Jill Levine: 'We translate to be translated.' Perhaps it is that: I translate because no one fully understands me.

On Translation: Two Letters and a Reflection

Ursula K Le Guin and Diana Bellessi

With translations from the Spanish by Leo Boix

A LETTER FROM URSULA K LE GUIN

She wrote me letters about my books, funny, crazy, fascinating letters I had to answer. We wrote back and forth. She made my letters crazy too, and I loved writing her. That was fun, that was easy. All words. I love words.

Then all of a sudden she writes, I'm coming to see you. I'm arriving from Florida on the plane. Now I was scared. Now it wasn't a game of words any more, now it was a person, some crazy poet from Argentina flying into my life, disarranging me. What do I do with her, what do I say to her, what does she want from me? I'm in the middle of a book and I don't want to stop for a stranger. She thinks she's coming to see the dream-hero she's made me into in her mind, and she'll find a middle-aged housewife who's afraid of people, shy, selfish, no kind of hero, and she'll be disappointed, I'll let her down, oh, why is she coming?

I knew her the moment I saw her among the people coming off the plane, tawny, a small puma woman, beautiful, with a beautiful smile full of diffidence and pain.

We talked, we read our poems to each other. She laughed easily, she cried easily, she read her poetry in her lovely husky voice. We have met twice again since then, laughed and cried and read poetry. We always write, but our letters get lost because the Argentinian

Post Office does something with them other than delivering them, and so half the time we don't know how things are going with the other one. Usually it goes along pretty much the same here with me, but in Argentina things have been bad, there have been times I worried about her, not hearing, not knowing. We send registered letters saying Dear One are you all right?

I learned French well long ago, Italian not so well. All the little Spanish I know I taught myself from books. Late in life I discovered that I could stumble along through Spanish translations of my own novels. So I tried Diana's compatriot Jorge Luís Borges, with the dictionary at hand, and soon cried Aha! How clever I am! I can read Spanish! But then I tried other writers, and found I was not so clever. Is it because Borges spoke English before Spanish that his writing is so lucid to us, or is it the great purity of his diction? I don't know. I do know that I still don't know Spanish, that Neruda is very hard for me to read and Gabriela Mistral is very very hard for me to read, that I cannot speak the language, and that I have no right at all to translate from it.

But I began to play with Diana's poems, just to see if I could understand them, for my own pleasure. She had been translating some of my poems, and I longed to be able at least to read hers. Though all her later books were far beyond me, their allusive usage and syntactic subtlety demanding a true, intimate knowledge of her Argentinian Spanish, I found to my great joy that the first two were accessible if I was methodical about looking up the words. I got a better Spanish-English dictionary and set to making English versions.

Translating is a way of making a foreign-language poem part of yourself. Spanish isn't the only language I don't know that I have translated from. This sounds foolish or boastful. I'm not Ezra Pound. What I mean is, I read the extant translations, and sometimes none of them seems quite right, so I begin to collate and change them, referring back to the original to pick up any words, repetitions, echoes, resonances that I can. I have done this with Lao Tzu for years (and have finally begun to do it methodically.) I have done it with Rilke. The Macintyre translation of the Duino Elegies is the only one I can stand; the others all seem more interference than transference. Rilke's French poems I could and did genuinely translate, but I don't know German at all, and so with several of the Elegies I have used Macintyre as a guide to making, not a translation, but my own private Rilke. I think this is a legitimate exercise. So, since I knew Spanish better than I do German, and a whole lot better than I do Ancient Chinese, I thought maybe I could get at Diana's poems in the same way, even without any translation as a guide.

I fell in love with them at once, and went on scribbling translations, every line a discovery, a shock of surprise and satisfaction. Nothing so restores the miraculousness of language as reading real poetry in a language you don't really know. It's like being two years old again. The words blaze out, they live lives of their own, mysterious, amazing.

I confessed to Diana what I was doing, and began to send her my scribbles. She sent them back with suggestions and explanations. She set my verbs straight when I thought *hear* meant *sit*, or got the right verb in the wrong person, tense, and number. It's not so much fun, maybe, being chewed up by the two-year-old. But she was joyously patient, and I blundered joyously on.

I would never have shown my versions to anyone but her, let alone print them, if she had not worked on them with me (always through the maddening unreliable mail), correcting, suggesting, and finally approving. These translations – hers of me, mine of her – are collaborations in the truest sense of the word. We worked together.

Crucero Ecuatorial is a very young book, and I love the young Diana who wrote it, long before I knew her – this little lioness going lithe and fearless along the roads of the Americas, looking at old Nazis and young fishermen and Peruvian prizefighters, laughing, sleeping in ancient sacred places, seeing the 'cracked, bare, quick, flat' feet of the fieldworkers, seeing everything tenderly and calmly with her golden eyes.

Tributo del Mudo comes from troubled times and was written, though only a couple of years later, by a maturer woman. The delicate Chinese echoes of its first pieces lead to increasingly rich, powerful, complex work, which I have found, as I worked on it over and over, to be inexhaustibly satisfying.

Translating is an excellent test of a poem. Sometimes they wear thin as you rub and polish and scrape and adjust your version. None of the later poems in *Tributo* have worn thin; they have only grown in nuance and resonance as I grow able to go deeper into them. The political terror of the years when they were written is touched on only by the lightest allusions in the second part, but like a drop of red dye those few lines colour and darken the whole book. The passion and strangeness of the dream poems in the third part leads on to the radiant intensity of the love poems and the earthy-transcendent splendour of the final and my favorite, 'Isla'.

Gracias, mi puma de oro, por el regalo de tu poesía y de tu corazón.

– Tu osita vieja

A LETTER FROM DIANA BELLESSI

My dear, it is a sweet October morning, a sleepy Sunday morning on the still, silent streets. I go for a walk, and my steps lead me to the green, first the Bótanico and then the 'forest'; that's what we call these parks: Palermo's woods. When I left the island and anchored in the city, I got as close to those trees as I could, but now it's been months since I've been here. Every day I go out to watch the trees around my house. I see the first greenery emerging, delicate filigree, almost invisible, and their magical, extraordinary growth, in wreaths of leaves whose variety never ceases to amaze me. Let me name them in my language: fresnos (ash trees), arces (maples), plátanos (plane trees), paraísos (paradises); they are the ones that abound in the streets, and suddenly a (tilo) lime tree, a Judea tree, the aura of a sauce (willow). I have walked these weeks under the inebriation of paradises in bloom, stopped in front of the unique rose of the lapacho trees, and there will still come the blue jacarandas of November when the avenues look like a spilt sea, and then the tipas with their yellow glow.

My steps lead me to the Forest, and already there, as at other times, I cry. With inexpressible happiness. Without understanding why I'm moving away from here. Everything I've done in my life has been to get away from it, to return to it; the green. Whilst sitting in the teahouse, drinking the golden green with rice, two giant cats lurk on the short artificial hill of the Japanese garden: one black and the other white, perfect, jumping as if in a dream.

My only One: you were not your characters for me; you were the whole Forest. The first letter I sent you in October, fifteen years ago, when I was still living on the island, was more than a letter: a little box thrown into the air across the continent to the address of a small publishing house in California, Capra, where you had published *Wild Angels*, a book I brought back with me from a trip. It all started with poetry, you see. I'll never finish thanking whoever passed it on to you. The little box bore the velvety, dark gold buds that hold the leaves of the plane trees; when they burst and fall gently the little leaves are released into the air. They have a musky, intense smell. They were the jewels that I sent you from the Paraná. A note said, 'What are you doing to me?' You answered me immediately with another little box containing a small branch from the Oregon desert, also intensely perfumed.

The almost wordless, pure materiality of the world we both love. But to think that it all started through your words. I've read everything you've ever written, did you know that? And I still long for your originals. No, you were never your characters. You were the Forest, and I, your characters. Simultaneously, you were a person who wrote those marvellous books, who understood me in such a way, who still knows. You had found your female reader. In my mind, I imbued you with all wisdom and all adventure. And I still believe you possess it.

Today, you are also my friend, my big sister of the North and also my 'Twin inside the Dream'. I knew that I had the unconscious strength of the Fool: you were creating distant worlds, and I was travelling to them, mind and body, to touch them. You were writing extraordinary stories, while I could barely put into words places and stories I had been to in person, to capture something faint in the vast hiatus of the poem. The silence was interrupted by a sliver of language. To name what? The Forest, and to return to it. The Forest which you unfold luxuriously before my eyes when you narrate, and which escapes with its mysterious touch in your poems – above all those I love most. That's how I began to translate you: to enter there.

Was it all words to begin with? Perhaps. Then I forced our meeting, and it wasn't miserable; it was beautiful. We became complete people. We became responsible for our love, and there was room for Charles, Elizabeth, Caroline, Theo, the cats, your house, and the Forest next to your home. And the ranch in the Napa

Valley where you translated *Crucero*, your brothers, your mother, and your father. I cried listening to Ishi's voice in the museum in Berkeley. My friend, it has been verbal, and we do not know what resonates of the rivers of the mind and heart in the words.

I will tell you now what I think about translating poetry when, as in our case, we choose the one who speaks to us to make her speak. It becomes, perhaps, the closest experience to the poem's writing; it is carried out in a slow process of self-absorption and silence, weighed simultaneously by the sonorous mass of a song, of a speech originating in a language other than the mother tongue.

Channelling through one's own emotion the thoughts and feelings of a foreign voice.

The poet recognises something in her writing when, in saying 'I', she feels she is uttering a voice that is both close and, at the same time, distant. She feels she is translating into herself something that seems to come from far away in time. If the poem appears first as a rhythm and only later in its own way unfolds meanings, translation is an effort of alterity. The alterity of the body breathing the music of another language and in the strict particularity of a voice that speaks it.

A double effort founded, no doubt, on love and the aspects that allow the translator to identify with various things. An echo, not a replicant, as in the myth of Narcissus, but sustained by the possibilities and mysteries of the mother tongue in which the translator rewrites it. To feel the text with the alert body at the same time of its significance, so that it unfolds in a language where it was not conceived, something – which is always something else – of that rose full of meaning that the original offers. Perhaps that is why the translation of poetry is more 'intuitive' and less derivative and logical than other translation tasks. Finally, it is always a meditation on one's own tongue and language itself since, if translating is to disarticulate the original, questioning the security of the meanings surrounding us, it is also related to our own language, as Walter Benjamin and Paul de Man put it. Poetry as a genre performs this act of doubt, even in its original language, in the most radicalised way. What, then, is its translation? Feelings of betrayal and, at the same time, the joy of reconstruction. Simultaneous mimicry and rupture, in other words, an almost impossible gesture. A gesture matured in a long previous coexistence, in an intimacy of souls where it's all about the written word, that sonorous carnality which perches on silence, that sequence of signs on the empty space.

I salute the beauty that your poems still possess in Spanish, a generous and wise language, nourished by the countries of the South that speak it with its tributaries of Quechua, Aymara, Mapudungun, Guaraní…, with their Italian resonances here in Argentina. I salute them, and I know how many echoes have been lost in translation, echoes full of meaning that every word and every syntactic or sonorous game brings in its original language. I know of the impossible gesture that all translation is, and even more of the poem that pretends to be almost pure materiality, the Forest itself. There I lose you, where I go to look for you. Yet our book has been our greatest gesture of mutual love which rests in a gesture of alterity, of letting be – in words – the other woman.

May the waters of the Klamath and the Paraná shelter our words, and may they turn them into the murmur of water from the same continent, without oppression or tutelage, like the twins they are, sailing towards the great river.

– Lovingly, your puma

A REFLECTION BY DIANA BELLESSI

Today, Saturday, the 29th of April 2023, my young friend Cecilia Paccazochi came to visit. She joyfully entered my house, bringing a book of Ursula K Le Guin's complete poems. She had opened it randomly on the bus on page 325, where she found the poem 'Hexagram 49'[1], which goes like this:

> How could I not love her? She
> wants what cannot be
> owned, or known, or gone;
> the way she seeks to find
> is the other one; the me
> she hunts does not exist, her
> 'baby, mother, friend, sister,'
> purer, stronger than ever I
> or woman was, her 'interlocutor
> in the secret rivers of the mind.'
>
> She transforms all to forest.
> She shames the owning, knowing,
> gaining of an end, she shines
> incandescent, without compromise.
> All that was and will be lost
> is golden in the puma's eyes.
>
> The fire in the secret river.
> How could I not love her?

The collection to which it belongs, *Sixty Odd*[2], was published a year after *The Twins, The Dream*. Later, Cecilia and I found the copy of the book which Ursula had sent me, complete with the dedication: 'To my golden puma, with love and gratitude, from

---

1   Ursula K. Le Guin, *Collected poems*, Library of America (2023).

2   *Sixty Odd*, Shambhala Publications (1999).

her old bear, Ursula.' On page 15, where the poem appears, there is the following message in her handwriting: 'You know that this is your poem.' 'Hexagram 49' is in dialogue with our letters, and rereading it surprised me as much as the photo in her film *The Worlds of Ursula K Le Guin*. Rediscovering that poem made me reread our letters as if they were written yesterday.

It would be simpler if I were not a lesbian to talk about this love story for what it was. 'How could I not love her?' says Ursula in her poem, and I could repeat it. We were two women who loved each other without touching each other. 'It has been by word of mouth, and we do not know what resounds from the rivers of the mind and heart in the words,' I wrote to her in my letter. As Ursula says in her poem, we were interlocutors in the secret rivers of the mind.

I was inspired to meet her because of *Wild Angels*, the 1974 collection of her early poems, but immediately after, I read her prose: *The Lost Hand of Darkness* and later, *The Word for World is Forest*. The impact of the latter book whilst I was living in the bush on the Paraná River made me write to Capra Press, Ursula's publisher. This is when I began to translate her, to enter the Forest that she was unfolding before my reader's eyes. This is also how I discovered the books of her mother Theodora Kroeber, and how I got closer to all that she loved. When I translated her poetry, I did it through the echoes of her narrative and from her voice, imitating the crows of Oregon. I was not her translator; I was her twin, with a 30-year age difference.

The translator, if they are able to choose who will make them speak – and this is the paradox which disrupts the image of them as merely a ventriloquist, a passive, obedient hand, in the colonial mode – if they are able to choose, and yet not force their own will on the text – a challenge faced by some male translators of poems written by women – then they have the possibility to construct a region that is truly expansive and on which they may insist their whole life.

Translating is also an extension of a prior gesture: reading. And it is the collection of readings accumulated throughout the poet's life that constitutes that lineage in permanent transformation. In those roots and in that trail which accompanies us, which contextualises us, I can pay homage and, at the same time, make visible a debt of love and knowledge to the American female poets who have occupied my days in reading and translation. Among them, you, my beloved little bear, until forever,

– Your golden puma

i-juca piranha

Érica Zíngano

Translated from the Portuguese by Francisco Vilhena

This poem is part of a longer work-in-progress, a playful dissection of the interstices of language, violence and colonialism.

piranha (etim. - *peixe dentado*) (s.) – PIRANHA,
o mesmo que pirãîa (v.) (Lisboa, *Hist.
Anim. e Árv. Do Maranhão*, fl. 173)
PIRANHA, tisoura; peixe de dentes muito
cortantes.

PIR-ANHA. Ictiologia: piranha, peixe da
família dos caracídeos, gênero Pygocentrus.
= pir-ãia. Substantivo (peixe-dentes afiados,
por analogia): + tesoura

i remember this one teacher
a french teacher ticiana melo
a very sweet teacher
many years ago this
back when we were on a placement
me and mirna juliana
my placement colleague
or maybe it was a different subject
before the placement

when we were getting ready
to start teaching french
as a foreign language
in order to be certified to teach french
as a foreign language
– one of the aspects of my education
in letters that i have fortunately set aside –
i remember her saying that

the methods for teaching a foreign
language
carry a certain historicity
and the audiolingual method for example
also known as
audiovisual
which was first developed
before the second world war
had been developed
as a war technology

it also became known as
army specialized training program
based on behaviourist theories
and repetitions elaborated in laboratories
i also remember her talking

about the vietnam war
and how before it was ever used in a classroom
as a didactic tool
to improve or potentialise
the learning process
of a certain foreign language
it had been used

– this she explained –
to train american soldiers
so that they would learn
in the most efficient and efficacious way
the language of those
they were about to kill
that year – in truth it was 2019
the year i began writing
this text – i began studying
tupi using navarro's method
modern method of ancient tupi
together with a study group from ufc
taught in self-managed mode
by teacher suene honorato[1]
and other interested parties

i am really very behind
compared to the rest of the group
it feels that i
am spending centuries
on the same lesson four
because of course
it has been kinda complicated
for me
to be able to reconcile
the learning
of an ancient language
with the unresolved
of my present existence
but life is funny that way
and it all gets mixed up
without us even really
noticing

ever since i moved back to brazil
i've been living in a street called
father luís figueira
– i'm not staying there any more
i just need to terminate the contract
and hand over the keys
i lived there for a little over a year
and then decided to move here to aquiraz
during the pandemic –
and father luís figueira
i did some research back then
just for the sake of it
mere curiosity really
i found that he
just like josé de anchieta
they wrote works about tupi
they were the first ones to write
grammatical arts of the language of brazil

i went to look for those works[2]
the pdfs of those works on the internet
i found and downloaded
facsimile editions of those works
and i started reading the pdfs:
grammatical art of the language most
used in 1595 on the coast of brazil
produced by the priest joseph of anchieta
of the company of jesus
and the 1795 grammatical art of the language
of brazil, composed by
f. luiz figueira

given that i was studying tupi
i was interested in understanding especially

how that language was systematised by them
during that period of colonisation

at the beginning   it's a little hard to read
because the portuguese is old
with that 1500-style calligraphy and its little circles
and also mixes many
expressions in latin
and it takes some time
to get accustomed to the stylus   because   of course
today we are much more used
to more communicative and dynamic
methods of learning languages
it's just that when we begin reading
these books
we find other things
other causes   causalities

in these books
we don't find dialogue
like this hypothesis
that might perhaps feature
in some ospb textbook
commemorating the day of the indigenous people

A: Hello! How are you?
My name is Tupi.
What is your name?
B: Guaraná!
Pleasure to meet you, Tupi!
A: The pleasure is mine, Guaraná!
B: Shall we play tapir and capybara?
A: Great idea! Let's do it!
I'll fetch my bow and arrow.

Whoever catches one first, wins.
B: Deal!

both anchieta's grammatical art
and luiz figueira's
present an overview of the language
in a very descriptive way
as if it were a linguistic treatise
that deals with the letters the nouns the pronouns
the rules of pronunciation and accentuation

and the first time   that both present us with
verbs in tupi
the first time they show us
how to conjugate the verbs
the verbs of the first conjugation in tupi
they don't use verbs
like the ones in the aforementioned hypothetical
    example
verbs we expect to learn
on a first lesson in any course
of any foreign language today
they use the verb to kill // jucâ / jucà
and they conjugate the verb to kill // jucâ / jucà
in every modality tense and person
corresponding to the portuguese of that time
with its respective translation in tupi

that choice of the verb to kill // jucâ / jucà
repeated in both grammatical arts
and in their reprints
does not appear to be   therefore   an innocent choice
an incoherent equivocation
or a simple road accident

of someone who is writing a book and distractedly
in the lapse of a second
turns away from explaining something
on the contrary   that choice they both made
for the verb to kill // jucâ / jucà
appears to want to illustrate
what actually is evidenced
immediately in the two grammatical arts
in writing those grammatical arts
which certainly served
to teach other people to learn tupi
portuguese people in this case
because   if we imagine that indigenous people
already spoke tupi
they didn't need to consult
those manuals
to learn to speak
their own language
the choice of the verb to kill // jucâ / jucà
really appears to reiterate
what has been proven
by the undeniable facts of history:
an ample extermination programme
genocide   since the colonial era

in this way   at the same time
those two grammatical arts operate
on two fronts
1) they function as textbooks
war manuals
that teach how to kill the other
in the other's language
a-jucâ / a-jucà: i kill, killed, killed
have killed, or had killed (would have killed)

where you are from mister understand that y-jucà-piráma
means: to be killed; thing that will have to be
killed; worthy of being killed
2) they work as testament
where we hear a mea-culpa confession
a-jucâ / a-jucà: i kill, i killed, i killed
have killed, or had killed (would have killed)
where one can also hear gonçalves dias
himself killing y-jucà-piráma
in both cases   these two documents
timelessly historical
are eyewitnesses
of the killing
aîuká-matutenhē
aporoîuká
îukába

after reading these grammatical
arts all i know is that   jucá
the jucá tree   caesalpinia ferrea libidibia ferrea
caesalpinia leiostachya
pau-ferro etc.   native of the mata atlântica
brazilian   ironwood   extremely hard
raw material of tacapes   clubs
batons   ibirapemas   iverapemes
of the indigenous
that tree   also known as
brazilian ebony
was never the same again
at least for me

Notes

1   In 2022, Prof. Suene Honorato, from the Federal University of Ceará, participated in the international colloquium, *History and Future of the 1922 Modern Art Week*, which took place at Unicamp. She gave the lecture '"Be tupi": anthropophagic contrasts in Ellen Lima's poetry'. Thinking about identity issues, she analysed some of these anthropophagic contrasts in Ixé ygara returning to *'y'kûa* (2021), Ellen Lima's debut poetry collection. Lima is an indigenous author born in Rio de Janeiro, of Wassu Cocal descent from the state of Alagoas. Suene Honorato also took a tour of issues involving tupinology in Brazil, a science loaded with ideological markers of cultural hierarchy, seeking to point out the historical controversies surrounding this language. Her participation in the Colloquium can be found in Portuguese on YouTube (https://www.youtube.com/watch?v=Ht-N6WobgOw); her lecture was translated into English, '"Be tupi": anthropophagic contrasts in Ellen Lima's poetry', and published in *The Living Commons Collective Magazine*: (https://livingcommons .squarespace.com/laura-harris_modernismo-1).

2   José de Anchieta's *Art* was first published in 1595, but as early as 1556 a handwritten version was already circulating: *Arte de grammatica da lingoa mais usada na costa do Brasil* (*Grammatical art of the most used language on the coast of Brazil*). Figueira's was reissued several times between the seventeenth and the nineteenth centuries, despite the precise date of the first edition of *Arte da lingua brasílica* not being known, and there not existing copies of the third edition from 1754. The other editions present some variations, as well as errors: *Arte da grammatica da lingua brasilica* (1687), *Arte da grammatica da língua do Brasil* (1795), *Grammatica da língua geral dos índios do Brasil* (1851), reprinted for the first time in South America, such a long time after its initial publication in Lisbon, offered to His Imperial Majesty by João Joaquim da Silva Guimarães; *Arte da grammatica da lingua brasilica* (1878); *Der Sprachstoff der brasilianischen Grammatik des Luis Figueira* (1899).

The Calling to Write Poetry in an Indigenous Language

Víctor Terán

Translated from the Spanish and Isthmus Zapotec by Shook

I was born in the city of Juchitán de Zaragoza, Oaxaca, Mexico, located in the region of the Isthmus of Tehuantepec, which is the narrowest strip of the Mexican Republic, between the Pacific and Atlantic oceans. Shared among the states of Oaxaca, Chiapas, Tabasco and Veracruz, it boasts one of the greatest Indigenous presences in the country, home to the Zapotecs, Ikoots, Mixes, Chontales, and Zoques. I was born, then, in a town baptised by the Nahuas (Aztecs) as Ixtaxochitlán, which over time became Juchitán, and which we Binnizá ('binni': people; 'za': clouds; 'Binnizá': people of the clouds) call Guidxiguie'quichi'. It means the same thing in both Nahuatl and Zapotec: Place of the White Flowers.

My mother tongue is Diidxazá, or Zapotec, and according to linguists it arose about 4,500 years ago from the Oto-Manguean language family. It currently has half a million speakers across 58 recognized variants with varying degrees of mutual intelligibility, divided into three major regions in Oaxaca: the Northern and Southern Sierras, the Central Valleys, and the Isthmus of Tehuantepec. Of our origins, it is said that the Binigula'sa, the ancestors of the current Binnizá or Zapotec race, 'descended from the clouds in the form of beautiful birds, with colourful plumage and strange, melodious songs… They were the bravest warriors and the most illustrious priests, they were tall and some say they were gigantic in size. They were magicians, doctors, and fortune tellers, and they knew how to read the whims of the future in the starry skies'[1].

From the Central Valleys of Oaxaca, the Zapotec king Cosijopí arrived to the Isthmus of Tehuantepec to found Juchitán in the year 1480 of the Christian calendar, and we have carried on and made our lives with sweat and love, that our history, culture, and language reveal what we are: a town of peasants, fishermen, artisans, and city workers who eat baked armadillos, iguanas, rabbits, and chachalacas, who eat red mole with shrimp or beef or pork, spicy iguana stew, and drink hot chocolate with marquesote, plain atole, bupu (atole with foam), and corn atole. I come from a place where women are embroiderers of beautiful regional costumes, and owners of the market and commerce. Where homosexuals are not discriminated against for their sexual preference. Where creators of art are born in bulk. Where we venerate and live with our dead on Todos Santos and on Palm Sunday. Where we love and celebrate the gods or our holy protectors with parties that last all night, called Velas.

I am from this place, and I share with you my experience as a poet. I was born in 1958 and lived in Juchitán until I was eleven years old. In 1969 I was taken to live in Mexico City, where I completed the last year of my primary education, as well as all my training to become a high school teacher. I knew almost no Spanish when I arrived in the Federal District. Since I couldn't speak Spanish fluently, I didn't make any friends, and since no one around me spoke Zapotec, which was the language I was fluent in, I began to talk to myself in my language, writing in notebooks, which later became the basis of my first book of poems. As you can see, I am a poet by destiny and I was shaped as an autodidact. I had no academic literary training – I was shaped by

1   Wilfrido C. Cruz, on the origin of the Zapotec, taken from his book *El Tonalamatl zapoteco*, published in 1935, translated here by Shook.

nostalgia and the desire to express myself to others, or to allow them to participate in life's anguish and joy.

*

I started writing poems out of nostalgia, a nostalgia caused by the distance from my town and my loved ones. And I decided to write in verse, because since childhood I had been passionate about reading the collections of poems at the library where I ended up living in Mexico City. There I met Juan de Dios Peza, Amado Nervo, Rosario Castellanos, Jaime Sabines, Xavier Villaurrutia, Gabriela Mistral, Pablo Neruda, and others. And also because in my childhood my mother told me stories from the Zapotec oral tradition and sang to me every night a pre-Hispanic poem about The Great Flood:

> Puumpu, capuumpu ¡au!
> ziaba nisa, ziaba guie
> ziaba nanda, ziaba yu
> Puumpu, ca puumpu, ¡au!
> ma chiguixiá guidxilayú

> Pitcher, the pitchers, au!
> it will rain water, it will rain stones
> the cold will come, it will rain ashes
> Pitcher, the pitchers, au!
> the end of the world is nigh

and the lines:

> Beeu, beeu Santa Rosa,
> para zé'na lia Rosa?
> Zicaa chupa ndaa gui.
> Xi guni gui?
> Cha'nde'xuba'.

121

Xi guni xuba'?
Gaca huana…

Moon, moon of Santa Rosa,
where did Mrs. Rosa go?
She went out for two logs of firewood.
What's the firewood for?
To cook the corn.
What's the corn for?
To make tortillas…

Images that never leave me and that shaped me into a sensitive, melancholic, romantic man. And, so, I found in the form of the poem how I could express myself, to make others feel and live what I felt and lived.

My longing for my hometown and my people inspired poems like 'Binnihuala'dxi'nga Naa', which begins:

Binnihuala'dxi'nga naa,
gule'ndaani'Guidxiguie',
rini xti'ca gula'sa'neá'
ne ludxe'ruunda'diidxaguie'.

Nanna'xi neza zaya'
ne nanna'pa raa nga zeaa',
neca guiaba guí zindaya',
rini xti'binnibisiá neá'.

I am native to these lands,
I was born in Juchitán,
I carry Zapotec blood and my tongue
scatters the sweetness of its origin.

I know where I come from
and I know where I'm headed,
even in rain I'll arrive aflame,
my blood the blood of eagle-men.

Later the wasps of love that inflamed my young heart made me
sing:

LALU'

Ridxí' ne huaxhinni, lá lu'.
Siadó', huadxí, lu gueela'
nisi lá lu' riree xieque
ndaani' bichuga íque'
sica tuuxa zeguyoo
runi biniti guendabiaani',
nisi lá lu' riree chuuchi
lu ludxe'
sica benda ndaani' ná'
ti guuze'.

YOUR NAME

Day and night, your name.
In the morning, the afternoon, at dusk,
only your name spins
through my head
like a man straight-jacketed
for having lost his mind,
only your name slips
over my tongue
like a fish between the hands
of a fisherman.

And the struggles of my people for democracy and justice made me write poems of protest like the following:

XAVIZENDE, BADUDXAAPA'HUIINI'RUDXEELA'

Xavizende,
badudxaapa'huiini'rudxeela',
guie'quichi'qui gapa xiladxi'
sica xpiaani'gubidxa,
guie'quichi'rindá'naxhi do'
sica ti le'xunaxi.
Nadxiee'lii
ti qui runibia'lu'guendanaguibi',
ti qui gannu'pa nuu guendarachelú sti'stobi.
Naro'ba'ladxido'lo', rudii nalu'tutiica;
pa chu'huaxa tu laa guchachaladi,
bisiá tica lii, ti guidxi beedxe'.

JUCHITÁN, MY BRIDE

Juchitán,
my bride,
white flower who spurns no one
like the light of the sun,
white flower with your heavenly scent
like a garden of virgins.
I love you
because you don't know avarice,
because you're unaware of envy.
Your goodness is enormous, you extend your hand to all;
but if someone unbecomingly takes advantage of your
    openness
you transform into an eagle, into a harsh village.

Why does Víctor Terán write in Zapotec, if it is a minority language, now in decline? I write in Diidxazá, or Zapotec, because it is the language I have mastered, the language I think in and explain my world in. It is my mother tongue, the language that gave me life. Does any writer write in a language he has not mastered? What is there to say without referring to a culture? A language is not just an alphabet and rules of grammar, it is most of all the customs and behaviour of society. Language is culture.

I write in the Zapotec language, then, to demonstrate that my language is as valuable and as complete, grammatically speaking, as any other language in the world. To prove it, I write. I write to defend my language from oblivion, so that it will not die, so that it will last until the end of the world. It is true that many Indigenous languages, like Zapotec, are in danger of disappearing due to the foolishness of those who govern the world, who think that Indigenous languages are a hindrance to development, and who don't hesitate to implement discriminatory and exterminatory policies to make them disappear. Hence the importance of writers in Indigenous languages, because they give life to their language and culture through the renovation of language: recovering and reviving old words, recreating and renewing existing words, creating new words – that is, saving their language from destruction and disappearance. Because, as Miguel León Portilla says, 'When a language dies / a window, a door / a glimpse / in a unique way / into what it is to be and life on earth / then closes / to all the world's peoples.' Writing, for us writers in Indigenous languages, is a cry of rebellion, an act of resistance and hope against the impoverishment of our peoples and against the disappearance of our languages and cultures.

My subjects as a poet are life, death, and love – what other themes are there in this world? I write about lucky and unlucky love, love interrupted at its midpoint like life by death, love like an overflowing pitcher that merciless luck shatters halfway along the journey. I sing and celebrate the fortune of living; I cry, scream, and impotently curse in the face of the injustices of a government that thinks only of business and money; I dream and fight for a better fate for my people and the peoples of the world.

My singing, then, is not only for readers in my language, but for the world, and I do it in free and occasionally rhymed verse. Don Carlos Montemayor said that my poems have a great musicality and conceptual precision; I say that it is the rich character of my Zapotec language that he describes. Indeed, Zapotec is tonal and poetry takes advantage of this tonal richness and sublimates it.

Translation is a consubstantial part of the writer in an Indigenous language, since he is obligated to translate his creations into the lingua franca, in my case Spanish, to reach a larger reading public and to be able to participate in calls for arts subsidies granted by the state. However, this does not mean that the Indigenous writer is an expert or even competent in translation, since much of the original is lost when transferring a poem to another language. That's why authors of renown say that translation is the art of the impossible.

It's true that 'poetic translation is the art of understanding not just the language but also the cultures: that of the translator, that of the author being translated, and that of those for whom it is translated'. For me, then, to translate is to build a bridge between two cultures, a bridge that allows us to come and go between two worlds. It's a glimpse through the awesome and enchanting window that is the original poem to continue living, dreaming, and suffering the author's experience in another language.

I will end by saying that literature, in addition to helping us feel and think about the everyday world from new perspectives, and to immortalising an experience or dream, keeps a language, a culture intact. Hence the importance of writers in Indigenous languages, who give life to their language and culture through their writings. Nonetheless, the writer's work is not enough to defend the continued presence and development of the Native languages of our country. In the face of the brutal onslaught by Spanish-language mass media and the educational and cultural policies of globalist governments, the children of the Native peoples of Mexico and the world lack the awareness of how to undertake the fight to defend our languages, by creating strategies that promote not only their survival, but also their development and enrichment. Meanwhile, writers in Indigenous languages will continue to fight: creating authentic and original literary works and raising our voices against the grievances committed against our peoples. In short, distinguished friends, Indigenous literature is a powerful instrument for the strengthening and renewal of Mexican languages and cultures.

BIGUIÉ'

Bi yooxho',
bi nanda,
bi guie'biguá,
bi gu'xhubidó':
Biguié'.

Ra lídxi ca gue'tu'cubi
zusichaahui'lu bidó':
zusiguaa xiiñibiduaa,
zanda cuananaxhi;
zacá beedxebiyé', naze guie'daana'
ne guie'biguá;
za'ta'daa, daapa cuananaxhi,
guendaró ne nisacha'hui'lú.

Gu'xhubidó', libana
ne tapa gui'ri'ro',
zusindá'naxhi ne zuzaani'
neza gueeda ne ché'
ca biuuza'gue'tu';
ca ni guedané ne chiné
ca ndaaya'rusieche'
laanu ne diuxi.

Bi guie'lubí,
bi gue'tu',
bi ndaaya',
bi ruaa bidó',
bi rusibani ne rusuí'
xpele gui'ri'guendanabani.

Victor Terán

FEAST OF THE DEAD

Impetuous primeval wind,
cold season,
of the scent of marigolds,
of exquisite incense:
feast of the dead.

In the house of the recently deceased
they adorn the saints' table:
raise banana trees
and decorate them with fruits;
the frame presides, lined with green leaves
and yellow marigolds;
in the center of the arrangement they will place the reed mat
brimming with fruits and delicacies.

Clouds of copal, prayers,
and four candles
perfume and illuminate
the path trodden by
the dead visitors,
who bring and take away
the blessings that drive
our life and god.

Scent of flowers in the air,
season of the dead,
of consecration,
breath of god,
breath that lights and snuffs
the candle flame that is life.

Translated by Shook

Part Four:
Subject and Context

On Tanka Form

Karan Kurose

Translated from the Japanese by Alan Cummings

In Japanese, I would say that I make my living as a kajin. Kajin are poets but ones who compose exclusively in the tanka form. There are various theories, but we can say that tanka is a form of Japanese poetry that began sometime around the eighth century. Of course, haiku are certainly the best-known form of Japanese poetry worldwide. The haiku form consists of 17 syllables in the pattern 5-7-5, whereas the tanka form consists of 31 syllables in the pattern 5-7-5-7-7[1]. This makes tanka shorter than most English poems but still 14 syllables longer than the extreme brevity of haiku. Due to this difference, haiku tend to focus on the depiction of nature, whereas the extra length of the tanka means that themes such as the emotional and psychological state of the poet or the passing of time are more common. If we were to compare the two forms to social media, then haiku with its momentary visual snapshots of the world would be like Instagram, whereas tanka with its use of the poet's emotions to gain the reader's sympathy would be more like Twitter (or do we have to call it X now?) That's my pet opinion, anyway – but, please, feel free to take it with a grain of salt.

Many years ago I was fortunate enough to have some drinks with Takashi Okai (one of the most accomplished tanka poets

1   Translator's note: I've used the word 'pattern' deliberately here, as in English we often think of haiku as a three-line poem and tanka as a five-line poem. However, in Japanese both are normally written in one single line with no punctuation or spaces between each phrase. Japanese readers therefore feel the breaks through rhythm and grammar, rather than perceiving them visually.

of the post-war period) and he shared a story with me. 'A foreign poet once asked me why Japanese people continue to write poems using words from 1,000 years ago, when there is no one in Europe who still writes poetry in Latin. I thought to myself: you know you're right, we could definitely revisit the question of tradition in tanka from that perspective.' The conversation moved on before I could ask who that foreign poet was, which country they came from, and how Okai had replied to their question. But that foreign poet is correct that Japanese poetic forms like haiku and tanka do have the reputation of having been written in 'words from 1000 years ago'. A visitor from the United States once also told me as much to my face.

However, the foreign poet's question was not entirely well-founded. There certainly are poets who have written modern poems in Latin, like Jan Novák from the Czech Republic and Anna Elissa Radke from Germany. While I don't have many more details, that does suggest that there are still some Latin poems being written in the present day. No doubt you in Europe will know more about this than me. However, compared to the subtle grammatical structures of Latin, the archaic language used in Japanese tanka is vaguer, more problematic and honestly, more slippery.

The kind of archaic language or 'old Japanese' used by kajin in contemporary Japan is merely pretending to be old. It's a language that has been recreated since the Meiji period (1868–1912), when the samurai period ended and Japan's modern era began. In other words, it is a pseudo-classical language. Don't get me wrong, it's true that many contemporary Japanese kajin write their tanka using language that feels a little older than the Japanese we use in daily conversation. But at its root, it is contemporary conversational Japanese that has been dressed up to sound old with classical-sounding verb endings and auxiliary verbs. The mentality that underpins it is entirely contemporary.

Contemporary Japanese tanka therefore exists as a chimaera made up of the past and the present. But for me personally, I experience great joy in my daily weaving of poems from that chimeric language. It is not contemporary Japanese with its efficiency of communication, yet neither is it the language of the people of the distant past. The Japanese language of tanka and haiku floats in vague forms, untethered from any single historical period, and in it we can locate a poetic ethos where the spirits of different ages can connect in diverse ways.

立山に降り置ける雪を常夏に見れども飽かず神からならし

The snow
That lies on Mount Tateyama
Even in midsummer
I never tire of gazing upon it
Surely this is a sacred mountain

Ōtomo no Yakamochi

夕立の雲もとまらぬ夏の日のかたぶく山にひぐらしの声

Evening thunder clouds
Have passed by, unstopping:
The summer sun
Sinks towards the mountains
Where the cicadas sing

Princess Shokushi

雲の峰空に立つ日は餌をはこぶ蟻のなりはひいそがしきかな

On days when
Cloud peaks tower in the sky
For ants carrying food
How very busy their
Lives must be

Masaoka Shiki

平日の明るいうちからビール飲む　ごらんよビールこれが夏だよ

Drinking beer
When it's still light out
On a weekday:
Beer, take a look, please
That's the essence of summer

Okamoto Maho

Above are four tanka on the topic of summer. I can imagine that it is difficult to discern differences in the qualities of the Japanese used in each poem when they are translated into English. But even so, surely it is possible for the reader to appreciate, however vaguely, the spirit of each of the periods in which the poems were written. The first poem, for example, is by an eighth-century aristocrat called Ōtomo no Yakamochi (718?–785), who left the capital to travel to Toyama in the north of Japan to take up an official appointment. He gazes in awe upon Mount Tateyama with its crown of snow that remains unmelted even in midsummer, and there, in the presence of the majestic mountains and valleys, he feels the existence of the gods (or perhaps in this case, it might be more precise to say the

135

spirits of that place). Here we can feel the directness with which people of the past experienced nature.

The second tanka is by another aristocrat, an imperial princess called Shokushi (1149–1201), who lived in the second half of the 13th century. As she gazes at the twilight that follows a summer thunderstorm, she feels the inescapable passing of time. Underpinning her words is the Buddhist concept of *mujō* or impermanence. Summer passes by in the blink of an eye; in the same way, my life will pass by too. The specific species of cicada she mentions in her poem is the *higurashi* or *kanakana*. It's an unusual type that cries quietly and sadly in comparison to the deafening racket created by most other cicadas. Japanese associate the cry of this particular cicada with the evening.

The third poem is by the 19th-century reformer Masaoka Shiki (1867–1902), who ushered in the modernisation of tanka and who here contrasts the magnificence of the towering clouds with the work of tiny ants. Before the appearance of Shiki, tanka were governed by strict rules around the ways that words that indicated the season could be combined, as well as around the kinds of words that could be used in a poem. We can see this kind of combinatory rule in the images in Princess Shokushi's poem: summer, evening thunder clouds, and cicada. Shiki introduced new expressive ideas rooted in naturalism. In his poem, he projects the image of human beings onto the image of the busily working ants. It is here that we can see a truly modern poesy.

The final tanka is by a contemporary poet, Okamoto Maho, who was born in 1989. In it she personifies the beer she is drinking, speaking directly to it. Here, there is no description of the scene and it is the poet's monologue that becomes the poem. Her approach is witty and refreshing with a sense of the pleasures of consumer culture. There's even a pop tone to the poem that you could imagine being used in commercial copy by a beer manufacturer.

When you compare these tanka in this way, the four poems are completely different in terms of the spirit of the age that produced them, their social sensibilities, and their common sense. Perhaps you even begin to question whether they all should belong in the same subdivision of poetry called tanka. They may all share that same 31-syllable format, but the poesy contained within each poem shows very distinct differences. This scale of difference could exist just as easily, by the way, in four poems created in the same period.

Kajin in contemporary Japan play many roles: we review and research tanka, we lead workshops aimed at amateur tanka lovers, we act as judges at tanka contests. For several years I have worked for a national newspaper, the *Yomiuri Shimbun*, selecting poems sent in by readers for its regular tanka column. Every week, the newspaper receives several thousand. Some are by elderly readers and read like they were written playfully in place of a diary, while others read like abstract art and resist easy comprehension. Some are by fans in praise of their sporting heroes, while others present trenchant critiques of society and the government. In terms of its politics too, the field of contemporary tanka is diverse enough to encompass poems written out of love for the imperial institution and those that express faith in communism.

All of that variety is an effect of the power of the fixed form of tanka. Archaic and contemporary language, refined poetic phrases as well as the ever-shifting varieties of colloquial slang can fit equally within that single form, and in doing so be transformed into poetry. Whether the poet is an ancient from the distant past, a samurai from the Warring States period, an early modern village peasant, or one of us from our contemporary society, the tanka each has created all meet together in the same field, defined by the tanka form. Through the form, we in the contemporary world can transcend the background and sensibility of our age and attempt to create a poetic rapport with an infinite host of dead poets.

懐かしき死に会ふごとく少年は闇夜の熱き腕に抱かれ

Like meeting
A longed for death
A youth
On a moonless night,
Held in feverish arms

夢を見て生くるは罪か　白きカモメ真白き崖に溶けゆく朝を

Following a dream
Is it some kind of crime?
A morning when
White seagulls melt into
The white cliffs

「おつきなみづ」とわらひだす児を抱きあげて汀を歩むやや育
　つまで

'Big water!'
My child laughs out
Holding her to my chest
And walking along the shore
Till she grows up a little

I started composing tanka because I wanted to write about death.
I wrote the first poem above when I was around eighteen. My
first published volume was filled with these kinds of poems and
as I wandered through the tanka world I met various people,
including my partner and in 2011 I ended up accompanying her
when she went to study in London for a year. The second poem
was written then, as I gazed upon the white cliffs of Dover. This

poem was included in my third volume of tanka, which went on to win the Maekawa Samio Prize. Thanks to that, various kinds of tanka-related work started to come to me. The third poem comes from our time in Fukuoka, a city by the sea in southern Japan. It dates from the days of raising my daughter who was born in London. My fourth volume, including this poem, won the Wakayama Bokusui Prize. Bokusui was a poet who spent his life in constant motion. I was delighted to receive the prize that bears the name of this lifelong poetic wanderer, as a proof of the nomadic nature of my own poems. When I compare these three poems, even I find it hard to believe that they were written by the same person. I started out dealing with death but now my poems lean towards questioning the power of life. However, as a poetic form, tanka is capable of capturing serenely the continually fragmenting workings of our lives, of throwing together our complicated conceptions of time, and of illuminating the poet's soul. I can feel that even from overly dramatic swings of my own development as a poet. And that power is, I believe, the power of the fixed form.

At the start of this essay, I wrote about old words and archaic language, but if we can talk about tanka as a poetic form that has protected a certain tradition right up to the present day, then rather than the element of 'old words' surely it should be the element of the 5-7-5-7-7 immutable form that we should point to. It is precisely because tanka is not free, multi-line verse, because it is confined within the fixed form of a restrictive single line, that the accumulation of poems over a very long period of historical time has created the sense of an ongoing poetic sequence that continues to flow before us. It is permissible for us to locate ourselves at one end of this tidal current and that is the pleasure of composing tanka. It is also perhaps the reason why this particular poetic form has continued to exist for over 1,300 years. Of course, this is a tidal current that exists in Japanese, in a small island nation in East Asia, its scale much smaller than that of

English. But even then, no, perhaps for that very reason, we can say that even now tanka retains multiple possibilities for a globalising society. There are some who continue to compose enthusiastically those five-line English poems they call 'tanka', and this has become a widening window for reconsidering the value of the tanka form in a multilingual environment. The increasing number of non-classical Japanese tanka that are being translated into other languages also creates the possibility for new collisions of poesies.

These too are perhaps some of the joys that can be found by locating ourselves at one end of the tanka form's tidal current.

A Poem on My Gravestone: On Death, Being Minang, and First Love

Zar Mose

Translated from the Indonesian by Khairani Barokka

What happened to the bodies ignored in the 1980s HIV/AIDS crisis? Before their deaths, were there actions those bodies did not get to accomplish? These were the questions that emerged for me when I saw the VCT (Voluntary Counselling and Testing) banner. Before doing the test, I thought, if I'm positive, will I be like Bianca Rodriguez and Pray Tell from the television series *Pose*, who hid their HIV status from the people they loved? Or even more dire, would there be a Pray Tell for me, who would always visit their lover lying helplessly in a hospital, as the virus in the lover's body spread and became AIDS? Or, if I was lucky enough, could I be like Michael from the series *Tales of the City*, living fully in the warmth of their family's embrace?

Sapardi Djoko Damono passed away in July 2020. He died leaving a vast inheritance for Indonesian literature. His grave is fragrant with a continuously replenished stream of prayers and flowers. His poem 'In My Prayers' is carved into his gravestone. I write because I would like a poem of mine to be carved into my gravestone one day – like Sapardi. I feel that this is not something most people whose bodies were ignored in the 1980s HIV/AIDS crisis got to experience. They were buried en masse, without being able to choose what kind of grave they wanted. The truth is that when HIV/AIDS was first announced as an epidemic,

141

many bodies were rejected by cemeteries. The monster that not only took over bodies but also governmental structures globally, feasted on their life force, which had already been marked by the virus. In such times, death – a topic written about by most poets – is no longer a metaphor, but a danger looming before one's very eyes. In order to write, in a queer context, I had to have a place to escape to. I had to travel far away from my hometown, Batusangkar in West Sumatra. A small, homogenous town that elevates Minang Muslim traditions through a conservative lens. It is only in this way that I would be able to write a poem for my own gravestone.

I agree with Virginia Woolf that a woman requires 'a room of one's own' in order to write her thoughts. It seems to me this also applies to myself, as people who are women and/or queer are groups punished by patriarchal cultures. And I am aware it is a privilege of mine to have 'a room of one's own'. In Minang culture, there is a tradition called 'marantau', which literally means to leave one's homeland and go to another land. Every boy on the threshold of adulthood is advised to find their living in others' lands. As a Minang saying goes, Ka rantau tumbuah di hulu, babuah babungo alun, marantau bujang dahulu, di rumah baguno alun. This proverb reminds us that a young man who is still a bachelor must learn in other lands, in order to come home bringing benefits for their birthplace. Due to my achievements in high school, I received a golden ticket to go to university on the island of Java, in the city of Semarang, to be precise. Merantau (as it is called in Indonesian) turned into a tradition that whipped me into shape, so I could learn from a life associated with danger. Danger that slowly infiltrated my own room in which I expressed myself. In the end, the tradition of marantau turned into a gateway that thrust me into the ability to write poetry.

*

I am currently an English Literature major at Diponegoro University, Semarang. A path that introduced me to the names of dead writers – who, to the best of my knowledge, did not share my exact fears. Some of them died tragically by suicide, such as Mark Fisher, Sylvia Plath, Ernest Hemingway, and Anne Sexton. Each of them recorded their own anxieties, leaving behind some kind of signals that can be studied by similarly suicidal readers. In the university library, I have tried to find them: the writers who died of suicide due to their fear of living as a gay person with HIV. I would like to study *their* signals. However, my research did not lead to answers. Literature by queers with HIV didn't seem to attract the attention of academics on campus. I am reminded of a friend saying that dying by suicide seems more dignified than being found out as someone who lives with HIV/AIDS. For me, though, it's not about dignity. Suicide – when viewed in an anarchic way of thinking – is a form of self-authority. Whilst queers who did not survive the HIV/AIDS crisis are victims of a genocidal system.

I must admit that poetry had no meaning for me until I first experienced it for myself. In my second year of university, I experienced what it felt to have a life that holds you. I had a love affair with a man whose name in translation means 'Penyair', or 'Poet'. His name moved me to record our story for posterity in poetic form. With Poet, the night sky could be blue, and that made sense. I understood how the word 'sin' chased after the pages of our relationship. Sadness and anger could not, in fact, be avoided. In difficult times I could freeze time just so I could think about him, and in this way everything felt better. More than this, Poet didn't just make me fall in love ('falling', because our relationship was full of wounds incurred from collapse) but also opened my mind to the dark futures of queers in Indonesia. Poet is a man from a Chinese Catholic family. He was raised in a religious family – just like me, though I'm Muslim. We were brought together – uniting two such different experiences in terms of tradition.

143

But like most queers in Indonesia, we are only here for a short stay. Only borrowing time until the right time to leave and continue on with our lives. In that short amount of time, I decided to commemorate our stories in a secret poetry collection that I would one day gift him as a book. I began to write about Poet routinely. I lived through the days in order to assemble words that were apt and majestic enough to collect into a mosaic of our romance. What manifested my writing was that the translation of his name was 'Poet'. I am the manifestation of his mother's prayers. If someone asks who I am, I will answer that I am a poet. Meaning, I am the answer to the prayer inherent in his name.

The oxytocin hormone in my brain actively helped me complete all kinds of poems. When I was writing, I felt as though all the organs in my body worked like an orchestra. This sense of being one with someone had never felt as harmonious. I wrote full of joy, feeling butterflies flap their wings in my belly. Until one night – a night in which I dare say the sky was not black, but blue – we met for the last time. This romance wasn't working as we had hoped. The love that he conjured turned out to be weak, unable to focus solely on the love that I offered him. *Could my love be too much?* All of my feelings were broken. Our relationship ended before our manuscript could be completed.

*

Firstly, I had a room of my own. Secondly, I had already gained experience in love. Two significant elements that bolstered my artistic side. Yet, I have to say it is a shame that a room of one's own, in the sense Virginia Woolf meant, turns out not to apply for queer individuals. I realised this when I thought about publishing my work on social media. My safe space stretched only as far as the room of my kos. Publishing my work meant destroying the walls of that room. There would be several risks attached, if I was brave enough to publish my writing:

1. I could lose my friends
2. What if I was found out by my family?
3. People could bully me, call me 'bencong' or insult me
4. Conversion therapy and ruqyah were once introduced as the official policy of West Sumatran regional governmental laws. Someone like me could be targeted by them

I could not see a bright path waiting ahead if my poems were published.

It took quite a long time for me to be brave enough to publish my work. The feeling of wanting to be heard, the feeling of wanting to unload my sadness, overcame my anxieties. However, I still have to think of my safety. Firstly, I have to hide behind a pen name. My name is Salman Alfarisi. In order to hide, I use the name Zar Mose. Secondly, I must ensure that the metaphors I use are in a certain direction, and do not openly indicate romance between two men. This subterfuge is the only way to be heard, though it will be misunderstood. It is, in my opinion, enough to be heard. People have showered praises on my writing, and a few have even contacted me to ask whether I am all right, as my writing seems depressive. I have always assured them that these are just writings, and I am fine.

After a while it occurred to me to publish the poems I once wrote for Poet. I collected all the poems that were 'safe enough' to publish. Aside from reasons of safety, those poems were easier for publishers to accept. The manuscript was sent along, and I only had to await the editing process. Around one month later, I received a reply from the publisher with edits on my manuscript completed. This is when the war in my head began to agitate. Not one of those poems specifically described a relationship like mine was. Two men, in their early twenties, Catholic and Muslim, Chinese and Minang. Not one of those poems let on that the two of us could only meet at night, because we were afraid of getting caught. Not one of those poems said that our relationship could only exist because we were living far from the places we came from. Those poems seemed half-formed. Incomplete. I contacted my publisher, with the aim of asking for time to think about whether or not I would publish this poetry collection. I did not know that poetry also meant war.

During this time of contemplation, of mulling over my decision, I reread the novel *On Earth We're Briefly Gorgeous* by Ocean Vuong. One of his quotes moved me. 'Because freedom, I am told, is nothing but the distance between the hunter and its prey.' In this fear, I was nothing less than someone hunted. I thought that by publishing 'safe' poetry, I could be free of the grasp of evil things. However, this freedom was only a false space. Sooner or later, everything would come out. And, if people out there wouldn't be doing so, my own mind would haunt me, or even hurt my body. In the end, Ocean Vuong writes, 'To be gorgeous, you must first be seen, but to be seen allows you to be hunted.' In this short life, on this borrowed time, I still have the option to shine. But to shine means I must bravely accept the risks that may endanger me. I finally made that decision: to shine. So I collected all the poems I wasn't brave enough to show anyone, and decided to publish them. That is how my first book, *Galeri Hormonal* (*Hormonal Gallery*), was born. A birthing process that opened up a path to various feelings: joy, emptiness, falling, until I reached it: fear. Unending fear. In the public health centre, in a freezing and dark hallway, I clutched my poetry book, awaiting the test results. If I was positive (I was very certain of the test results), at least I had a poetry collection from which something could be engraved on my gravestone. I am reminded again of what a friend said, that suicide was more dignified than living with HIV. However it ends, I will have fulfilled my one wish before I die.

I would like to end this essay with another thought from Ocean Vuong, that queer poets do not have two roads – as Robert Frost wrote in his poem 'The Road Not Taken' – but only one. And that one road is strewn with wild shrubbery. I must traverse all the branches, cleanse the road of reeds, and, if I must, install lights all along the way. I look behind me, and there haven't been Minang poets like myself who have been brave enough to surface. I am sure they exist. But the road some journeyed on must have been so difficult that their names were not remembered. The footsteps of Chairil Anwar, Taufiq Ismail, Marah Rusli, or Afrizal Malna belong on the other road, one that I cannot even see, let alone walk along. We have the same Minang blood, but our blood does not spill on the same battlefield. If they die as poets, then I will die as a *poet*. What I mean is, I will die as the answer to the prayer in someone's name.

No Man is a Fern Plant: Writing in Isolation

Carla Diacov

Translated from the Portuguese by Annie McDermott

'No man is a fern plant, entire of itself' John Donne

He wasn't talking about writing in isolation, And Yet. It's within the And Yet that this essay resides.

And Yet.

Gustav Mahler composed *Das Lied von der Erde* (*The Song of the Earth*) in isolation, during a dark period, during what was known as the 'plague of the damned', which destroyed some of the damned in that region, at that time. You don't often hear of the 'plague of the damned', because the 'plague of the damned' never existed; I just invented it, and I don't know much about Mahler's life and work, either. And Yet. And Yet it's with that invention that I'm beginning my cursed text about writing, about creating in isolation.

What do I have to work through, to see and unsee/unthink from my almost ten years of isolation? Nothing, and this nothing amounts to a great mass of everything. I have the 'plague of the damned', I have everything I can when it comes to my ability to intervene, to tell lies, to open, fold, stretch out and shape that mass. A muse like that is a muscle that needs to be exercised. In isolation, the muse needs the whole world to run around in.

In my almost ten years of experience with a reduced world (in cooking and other kinds of essence extraction, reduction offers the exact opposite of what it says: it means containing everything essential within a tiny amount, having a sauce that says, in 'a few words', the same as a whole bottle of wine… Five millilitres of rosemary oil, the product of fifteen kilos of branches and leaves), I find it easy enough to have at my fingertips the totality of what lies beyond it, of experiences I've had, of experiences I've invented, and, when necessary, a magnifying glass held over this totality, expanding its concentrated form.

It was in total isolation that I wrote my book *The Menstruation of Valter Hugo Mãe*. I immersed myself in two books by Valter and the ultra-feminine atmosphere of my own menstrual blood, which I used to make drawings that influenced the poems in the book. Over two months and some days, I experienced that reduction and expansion of the subject matter. I had the essence, the worlds in Valter's books and my infinite little room of eleven metres squared. The book was born, with some pain and much pleasure; it was born and now it rests upon itself and I turn my isolation in the direction/intention of other creations, sometimes commissioned and sometimes not.

With my complete faith in perspective, I am the room and the window, in that I bring to the landscape whatever I want. I balance my sick head (depression, manias, emotional disorders, panic syndrome, agoraphobia, etc) between invention and transformation, between approximating and appropriating worlds. Making the idea, the discomfort, visible and palatable. Perhaps like a fern plant, its roots never leaving the pot even as it turns the sun's rays into internal flux, salvaging from the carbon dioxide some hope of transcription, translation, moving gradually through the days, unfurling new fronds of being. Or even, like my friend Gustav Mahler, making use of the isolation imposed by the 'plague of the damned', gathering himself before the leap, readying his stomata and setting off!

With the And Yet an immense arrow pointing towards movement!

Thinking about isolation is frightening, but as we know, as we know deep down, isolation is part of being in the world.

Writing in isolation means having the ideal creative conditions. But unlike isolating yourself in order to write, being a writer who, for health reasons, lives and works in isolation is also frightening and sometimes painful. I've learnt to make this situation into a pathway, a set of strategies for reconsidering the world.

I'd say I've had a fairly intimate relationship with isolation ever since I was a girl. I'm the only child of reserved parents. I didn't have many friends, in or out of school. I can confirm that most of my experiences of joy or wonder in life, the vast majority of those events, have taken place in isolation or near-isolation, with one or two people nearby or perhaps surrounded by people but nonetheless feeling isolated inside, which casts the as-yet unconfirmed suspicion of autism over my medical history. And what if we see this suspected autism, and my other mental and emotional conditions, almost as tools for my body, tools that allow me to find, in my isolation, ways of processing life? It makes sense. Neurodivergence is also about physical changes in the brain caused by particular events.

The fact is that in isolation I feel more authentic; I function better in my unruly, irregular daily life, which is customised to my needs. I trained in theatre, at a time when I was trying to leave this isolationist tendency behind, and yet even so, rebelliously, my creativity worked better when I was alone, becoming more fluid, more natural and truer to itself. With a bit of effort I managed to work in a team several times, and I think I'd still be able to do it, as I say, with some effort, and some pleasure.

During the Covid-19 pandemic, I was able to see the effects of isolation on others – on the people around me, on my neighbour, my friends, my mother. I find it astonishing how some people react to isolation, and it makes me very sad to see that, for many of the people I know, people who are very dear to me, isolation brings with it a heavy burden of sadness. And they then project this burden onto those, like me, for whom isolation is a companion, a friend, a good atmosphere and, in its various forms, something more or less comfortable, as comfortable as the lives of more sociable people.

In a conversation with my psychoanalyst I came out with the following phrase: *I feel like the Covid-19 pandemic made the world fit my life.* I felt bad right away, all over again, for the people around me, for the world, for the dead. What a horrible thing to say, to feel! I said it, of course, on a pretty selfish impulse. Now the outside world was more suited to my circumstances and fears, with its empty markets, masks and social distancing! Oh, social distancing! And the online world going full steam ahead! I could be with people without being in the same space as them thanks to online events, I could watch plays from the comfort and calm of my bedroom! The pandemic is over now and, to my selfish satisfaction, some of the adjustments that bring art to people in isolation remain! Here we have a very clear demonstration of what isolation can do. Isolated, And Yet! The individual as the owner of her doors and windows!

An aside to my selfish comments about the pandemic: might it not be in the unconditional defence of our own ideas that the seed of something genuinely authentic can sprout? Is this a very selfish way to think? To be honest, I think selfishness, particularly as a defence mechanism, actually has a lot to offer the practical, collective world. After all, what helps me to feel comfortable might help other people too.

The truth is that, within the limits of isolation, physical or internal, there are no limits at all, and this is definitely true for all those of us who, to a greater or lesser extent, need seclusion, precisely because seclusion is in itself the potential for expansion, both outside and inside ourselves.

The individual, as an individual, acquires meaning in the world first of all through isolation, through the contours and limits of the body, the world itself coming into being based on those first lines of self-understanding, on the organic machinery that chews up, deconstructs and replicates the outside world, turning it from *the* outside world into *our* outside world, now fully customised to suit our needs. With this in mind, perhaps going into isolation is also an act of filtering, of refining, of returning to the beginning and, who knows, of adjusting, disorganising and rearranging the parts of that machinery for seeing and being in the world. Of course, this is all the domain of the And Yet, the same And Yet that brought new ways of being to the world, and to life in society, during the Covid-19 pandemic.

The And Yet is made of something elastic, of inappropriate chemistry, of irritating workings. The And Yet is like dust, alive and suspended in isolation, subject to the whims of chance and sunsets, ready for the intimate inner safari of writing, of creating, of expanding our movements and even our bodies, without necessarily being visible or tangible.

John Donne was right: no man is an island – and yet.

Echoes of Love: Exploring Somali Literature and Personal Revelations

Xasan Daahir Ismaaciil 'Weedhsame'

Under the scorching sun, with the once-dry sands now a radiant oven, my friend Cabdiraxmaan Baas and I sought refuge in the shadow of a resilient building, bearing the scars of a long-past war. The world around us had transformed, leaving us parched and sweating. Little did I know that in this unexpected moment of heat and discomfort, Cabdiraxmaan would unveil a hidden talent that would inspire, captivate, and change my life forever. As we leaned against the weathered walls, he recited his own poetry – words infused with his deepest feelings, thoughts about life, love and hope. In that instant, under the relentless sun, his verses became a sanctuary, and I was entranced by the beauty of his creativity. Without hesitation, I confided in my friend, admitting that I too could write poetry, even though I had never attempted it before. In a surprising twist, he handed me a paper and pen, challenging me to craft a poem on the spot. To my amazement, the words flowed effortlessly from my pen, crafting a verse that left Cabdiraxmaan agape. With each revelation, Cabdiraxmaan repeated several times, 'Are you kidding me? Is it the first time you've written poetry?' The poetic exchange between friends, amidst both adversity and creativity, was a moment forever etched in our memories.

However, as I reflect on that day, an unsolved puzzle still lingers, defying my understanding. I penned a verse about unrequited love, an emotion I had never personally experienced. For a long time, I remained on a quest for answers, contemplating why such an unfamiliar and enigmatic topic wove itself into my early poetic creation. Simultaneously, I often found myself wondering about the identity of the girl in my subconscious, the one I loved and ardently wished to be my companion, who had left me with a mystery which compelled me to write a poem. These personal questions have brought me to another frontier, where I ponder the contrast between the way Somali males are raised, expecting them to be strong, and the way our literature depicts men in love.

The upbringing of the Somali male and the portrayal of men in love in Somali literature reveal a stark contrast. Somali culture places strong emphasis on avoiding expressions of vulnerability, a quality deeply ingrained in the Somali way of life. A Somali mother once shared a valuable life lesson with her son, advising, 'My son, you should never be the first to express three things before your peers: fear, tiredness, and thirst.' This way of life is not only a cultural expectation but also a deeply rooted belief. Somali boys are raised with a firm conviction in strength. Complaining or showing vulnerability is strongly discouraged, especially in the company of peers, and even more so in the presence of women.

The portrayal of men in love within Somali literature, meanwhile, could not be more different. In our songs, men in love are depicted as passionate, devoted, and willing to endure great hardships for the sake of love. Many Somali songs in which men express their love for their beloved ones are full of whining and complaints, a sharp contrast to the strong and resolute persona expected in our everyday lives.

This stark contrast between how the Somali male is raised – prioritising strength and stoicism — and the emotionally vulnerable portrayal of Somali men expressing love in literature can be explained by two fundamental aspects. The first is that literature serves as a channel for the expression of repressed emotions, providing a valuable space for individuals to navigate and process emotional experiences. This bridges the gap between the anticipated outward display of strength and the concealed emotional depth within individuals, allowing for the exploration, communication, and acknowledgment of these emotions, contributing to a more comprehensive understanding of the human experience.

The second aspect is the life and work of Cilmi Boodhari. The tragic love story of Cilmi and Hodan Cabdulle not only influenced our literature on love but also shaped our very concept of love. His poems, expressing the longing, heartbreak, loss, and unfulfilled yearning for his beloved Hodan, continue to echo today. Drawing on his experience, our perception of love became synonymous with profound suffering and rejection; an anguished lament resounds within the verses penned by successive generations of poets. Many poets following in his wake mirrored his path, sharing their own poignant and unrequited love stories, echoing the sorrow and pain found in Cilmi Boodhari's legacy. Cilmi's influence is vividly evident in the *Qaraami Songs*, the pioneering pieces of Somali modern music. These songs resonate with the voices of grieving lovers, despair, rejection, complaints, longing, and occasionally (albeit sparingly) dissatisfaction with their beloved ones – all of which suggests they are following in the footsteps of Hodan – the woman for whom Boodhari sacrificed his life.

Cilmi's depiction as a love martyr, a title befitting his legacy, is a motif that recurs in our verses. Nevertheless, beyond his romantic image, his literary works functioned as a platform to scrutinize and confront established beliefs, practices, and societal norms. His challenging critique of conventional standards sparked crucial developments in our community. Through his poetry, Cilmi facilitated the identification of biases and systemic imperfections deeply embedded in our culture, fostering an environment for introspection and transformation. He expressed dissatisfaction with the surprising ignorance among Somali peers concerning women's love and its significance to a man. In one of his poems, Cilmi protested fiercely, saying:

Soomaalidaa caado xune iguma caydeene
Oo ima canaanteen sidaan cuud ka iibsaday

The Somalis have awful customs, or you would not insult me.
You would not have scolded me as if I'd taken all your wealth.

I was mentored as a poet by Maxamed Xaashi Dhamac 'Gaarriye',
whose focus wasn't primarily on love poetry, even though he, like
his peers and predecessors, experienced heartbreak and unrequited love. The great Maxamed Ibraahin Warsame 'Hadraawi',
also, significantly influenced my perspective on love poetry.
Fortunately, I encountered his book *Halkaraan* early on and,
before delving into his politically themed poetry, which posed
linguistic and mental challenges at that time, I absorbed and committed to memory his expressions of love in poetry, savouring
every poignant verse, as if tasting the bittersweet essence of his
affections. Almost twenty percent of Hadraawi's book Halkaraan
consists of poems centred on unrequited love. What astonishes
me is that, during his time in prison, Hadraawi composed nine
poems, four of which express his yearning for someone who did
not reciprocate his feelings. It is truly remarkable that, despite
being in the clutches of a dictatorship that could have terminated
his life at any moment, Hadraawi's preoccupation with thoughts
of a woman diverted his attention from those dire situations. I
am still curious about the identity of that fortunate woman in
Hadraawi's thoughts, who represented for him respite from
the solitude and hardship of prison life. From my perspective,
Hadraawi emerges as the true inheritor of Cilmi Boodhari's
emotional depth, authentically reviving Cilmi's poignant voice
and sentiments. As one of the greatest disciples of Cilmi's school
of love, Hadraawi's eloquent poetry revitalised themes of unrequited love. More importantly, Hadraawi's love poetry served as
the umbilical cord that connected me to the world of poignant
love stories within Somali poetry.

In the spring of 2001, I was graced with the golden opportunity to meet Hadraawi, a moment I cherish to this day. It felt like a stroke of sheer luck as I presented a poem before this literary luminary. We were a cohort of young talents handpicked by Gaarriye from various secondary schools in Somaliland, all of us aspiring to be the future vanguards of poetry. Sadly, our initial recitations primarily revolved around political themes, failing to resonate with the discerning tastes of this distinguished wordsmith.

Once we concluded our recitations, Hadraawi himself took the stage. With a powerful presence, he articulated, 'Where are the verses of young hearts that sing of love? Where is the praise for the ethereal beauty of our princesses?' This declaration marked a significant shift in the thematic direction of my poetry.

Seven years later, I had the chance to reconnect with my literary idol Hadraawi, but this time, it was on a more personal level. Rashid Sheikh Cabdillaahi, a close friend of Hadraawi and one of the most esteemed Somali literary analysts, facilitated our meeting. It took place under the canopy of a tree near his office in Hargeisa. Rashid, brimming with enthusiasm, exclaimed, 'You'll be surprised when you hear this young man's poetry,' and encouraged me to share my work. I was astonished by his humble and approachable nature, despite his remarkable stature. I began reciting a poem 'Royal Jelly', recounting the story of a beautiful girl. He was delighted and completely captivated by the verse, urging me to continue line by line and expressing his joy by tapping the table enthusiastically. When I finished reciting the poem, he praised my eloquent poetry, filling me with an energy that would drive me for years to come. After that day, we often met whenever he visited Hargeisa. Whenever he laid eyes on me, he'd always say, 'Weedhsame, recite your new verse to me.'

In 2008, my heart tasted the bitter experience of unrequited love, which echoed in my writings. One day, as usual, Hadraawi requested that I recite my latest verse to him. I began reciting a song that forced me to open my wounded heart:

Haddii aan naruuriyo
Shalay idhi 'naq baad tahay'
Maantana nal baad tahay
Iyo nuurka aragtida,
Nasab qaaliyaad tahay
Qof naf loo huraad tahay
Hankaad naago dheer tahay.

Anigoo nacayb iyo
Naxli aanu igu jirin
Naso waan ku daayee,

Nabsigaygu kuma helo
Nin xun eebbe kuma bado
Nabaadiino inanyahay
Kollay nooli kulantee.

If yesterday, I said: you were good-fortune.
And exemplified the shine of green pastures
Today you are beauty personified
And the glow that gives sight
You are of noble lineage
A soul worthy of sacrificing oneself
And with ambition surpass the rest.

But without resentment or an ounce of loathing, I say:
Rest easy, I have let go
May ill fate not befall you!
And you be overlooked by cruel man
To you, peace!
The living do meet again.

158

With every line, I sensed the emotional weight cascading through the air, and Hadraawi's attentive silence was profound. His empathetic presence encouraged me to voice the unspoken depths of my heartache. He was a deeply compassionate individual, and I could feel how deeply this verse had touched him. As I delved into the profound chambers of my desolate heart, expressing the unremitting pain of unreciprocated love without restraint, it felt as though I was being buried alive by the intensity of that emotion. Hadraawi gazed at me with empathetic eyes, posing the question, 'Please, tell me there's a beautiful princess who inspired such a powerful verse.' Before I could respond, he reiterated several times, 'This surpasses mere imagination,' and he was right about that beloved princess.

As I've grown older, my view of unrequited love has evolved. Nowadays, I believe our fixation on glorifying unrequited love in verses may be driven by unexplored motivations and underlying causes. Recently, a knowledgeable friend of mine listened to one of my songs titled 'Separate Beings'. Noting the absence of a specific romantic interest in my life, he delved into the song's theme. His conclusion was intriguing: unrequited love, as depicted in my song, isn't solely about romantic relationships. Instead, it's a symbol of unattainability that extends to other life desires and goals. He proposed that the song hints at humanity's pursuit of what seems beyond reach, providing depth to the theme and connecting it to broader aspirations.

This realisation prompts me to consider the elusive identity of the girl in my subconscious as a representation of unfulfilled desires. The poetry on unrequited love acts as a mirror reflecting the dreams, hopes, and truths that often escape our conscious awareness.

CHUPAR LA PIEDRA

Al citrino lo chupo con cuatro lenguas la lengua de la palabra
la lengua de la salud
la lengua del frenesí
y la lengua del conocimiento
aparentemente una de las lenguas
está dividida en dos
tampoco la madarria tritura al lapislázuli
por el contrario
lo quiebra dulcemente y le da poderes húmedos
le da el don de los sueños
el don de la tierra
el don de las cuidades con límites y flora
nadie ve al lapislázuli debajo de mí
nadie me ve
por eso no la he chupado
aunque sé que la venturina tiene sabor a oxígeno
a mí carente de oxígeno
me falta eso que las muchachas llaman habilidades no soy
   habilidosa pero soy amorosa
y el emor es señal de sabiduría

Legna Rodríguez Iglesias

160

SUCKING THE STONE

I suck the citrine with four tongues   the tongue of language
the tongue of health
the tongue of frenzy
and the tongue of knowledge
apparently one of these tongues
is forked
the mallet does not pulverise lapis lazuli
on the contrary
it breaks it sweetly and gives it wet potencies
it gives it the gift of dreaming
the gift of earth
the gift of cities with outskirts and flora
no one sees the lapis lazuli underneath me
no one sees me at all
for this reason I have not sucked it
though I know that venturine tastes like oxygen
like my lack of oxygen
I lack what the girls call *skills*
I'm not skilled but I'm loving
and love is a sign of wisdom

Translated by Abigail Parry and Serafina Vick

Writing as a Woman; Or, Being a Woman Makes You Frown

Legna Rodríguez Iglesias

Translated from the Spanish by Serafina Vick

The mouths of the women we love are so lovely. Mouths of female friends and mouths of female family members. Mouths of women that speak, write, sing, think and represent things we like, things we agree with or simply that we're attracted to. Even the mouths of women we loved and no longer remember, mouths we try to recall in vain because we don't even remember the words that came out of them, they're also lovely, in their way.

When I speak with a woman my eyes are drawn to her mouth, unless there's something wrong with her mouth, or I don't much like her or she doesn't much like me and we're talking out of obligation or politeness. In this instance the woman doesn't even have a mouth, or a head or hands, which are another feminine boon, hands. In this instance there's something so lacking you have to interact on a rather precarious level of humanity.

In almost every photo my girlfriend, the Cuban photographer Evelyn Sosa, has taken of me, I'm frowning. I tend to purse my lips when I go to smile. I must be resistant to smiling, to happiness or love, even though I fall in love quick and hard. There's a resistance in my mouth, in that frown. It's not to say I don't want to be happy or don't want to fall in love, but rather I know its ephemeral conditions all too well, its difficulties of permanence, its levels of abstraction. Paradoxically, the less I frown, the less in love I am.

Evelyn takes photos of me frowning, facing her, for her. As we're two women who both like and desire one another, we watch each other's mouths constantly, as though our mouths were the only thing we desired in life. In fact, they're not the only thing. A woman is someone full of desires and full of hopes, just as she's full of clots and eggs, just as she's full of ideas and imagination, just as she's full of glands and ovaries. Long live the female imagination.

In fact, a woman is sometimes someone too brave to admit that she is. And so powerful and strong, even though she can't lift the same weight as a man, because it's true she can't. In my job I carry books from one place to another. I'm very proud of all the books I carry and pick up and deliver because, firstly, they're children's books, and secondly, they're for children who don't have access to books most of the time. We're moving office and they all need to be tidied into boxes. Medium-sized and big boxes. Books, computers, other electrical equipment and more books. Our manager met with us delivery drivers and there was only one female driver present at the meeting. Guess who. She came up to the female driver, which was me, and asked: would you rather go to Storage and lift boxes or stay here labelling?

My answer says a lot about me as a woman. I carried on labelling for two hours, making up my own weekly delivery of boxes. I didn't go to Storage with my driver friends, it was far too sunny and I prefer to lift boxes only when it's unavoidable. I'm also very proud of what I choose to do without. My strength is an invisible weight which I lift with invisible muscles.

A friend drew me eating cashews and having faith in the human race. The drawing is part of a four-handed book of poetry coming out with Ediciones Furtivas here in Miami. In the drawing, just like in the photos, I'm frowning. Cashews make your lips purse, make the palate sulk, scrape the teeth, but you keep on eating.

It was this same friend who decided to post the following:

> Deprived of sanitary towels, Cuban women, denied the right to peaceful protest against repression and the Cuban dictatorship, use rags. According to a wide range of international organisations menstrual hygiene is a human right, a right which has been denied to Cuban political prisoners and other inmates, resulting in a bloody menstrual indignity every month.
>
> Firstly, we demand that the dictatorship in Havana free female political prisoners. Secondly, a request to the international organisations promoting menstrual hygiene: take a look at Cuban prisons. Thirdly, we ask the expatriate Cuban community to create a network of direct help for the inmate-citizens, to guarantee the menstrual hygiene of political prisoners and other inmates.

When I read this I thought that this initiative could only come from a woman, because only women understand other women's needs with absolute accuracy. And I thought this communiqué represented the notion of being a woman: their strength and their intransigeance. And I remembered my pains and my cramps, every 30 days since I was 15. And I remembered the seven days of blood, first a stream and then a river.

At the weekend I bought a sofa so that my son and I could be more comfortable, because after signing a contract for another year's rent in which the price of the rent went up by more than 150 dollars a month, feeling comfortable is the least a woman deserves.

What I really wanted to write about was the women I've been with. I wanted to write about these women lying on my sofa. A blue sofa that matches the lamp. A two-seater sofa which I fit on

164

even if my feet stick out. I carried the sofa myself and stuffed it into the little Chevrolet Spark, then I carried it up the stairs, put it together and tightened the screws.

I've got the names of the women I've been with saved in a note on my phone, if I haven't deleted them. My girlfriend asked for their names a while ago and I tried to be honest. I remember feeling embarrassed. A woman is someone who can be embarrassed in front of other women, if she has a good reason to be. And I remember that I resisted asking my girlfriend the same question. I'm so different from her previous girlfriends.

I'm a writer interested in a carnivorous kind of writing, eating everything that's put in front of me. I'm interested in exhibitionist writing, lacking scruples and restraint. I'm a writer of books, not standalone texts. The only standalone texts I write are and will be the product of necessity, material and intellectual. I'm interested in conceptually corporeal projects, that is: made up of various organs, especially guts. I think about that solid, substantial part, its name and shape coming from its first extremity, its need for a second extremity, a third, a fourth. And so on and so on until it becomes a body.

I write standing up, sitting or lying down. I mention this because it shows. You can see my physical and moral state in my writing as I produce what might or might not be literature, and this intrigues me. I write badly, moderately or well, like a schoolchild. I'm interested in writing born of a (supposed) lack of knowledge, though not a (supposed) lack of truth. I'm interested in the virtue of experience. I'm interested just as much by language as by its annihilation. *A giant onomatopoeia.* I'm interested in the Spanish language, and writing in Spanish could be, now that I think about it, my true country. Writing from the perspective of a woman, mother and immigrant is also my true space. A space I have arrived in by choice.

I'm interested in illiterate writing (grammatically dirty, writing *in need of polishing*) just as I'm interested in biological writing, based on cells and internal proteins, based on substances, on guts, on threads of hair. Writing is working. Writing provokes hair loss.

Urinating, lubricating, salivating. Menstruating, ovulating, pushing, birthing, defecating, vomiting, crying: this makes up my body and this makes up my writing. A body and the writing of a woman, mother, *camagüeyana*[1] and unpeeled-loquat-eater. That's why the author photo for my reading with Raquel Salas Rivera at Arizona University could be of one thing only: me urinating.

I wonder about my son. I wonder what kind of woman he sees in me, because a woman is someone who's always wondering, wondering about things only she knows the answer to because she is made up of that answer. And I ask myself how my son will see me when he stands before me and looks at me the way he's yet to do, in an attempt to understand me.

I want him to look at my mouth even if I might be frowning at the time, out of embarrassment or pleasure or both. I'm sure that I'll purse my lips and half-smile. Since my pregnancy, the outline of my lips has been stained, so that now it's a stained mouth that sits on my face under my nose. Even stained, even frowning, I am a woman and this is *guánderful*.

1   from Camagüey, Legna's home town.

A City Called Exile

Azita Ghahreman

Translated from the Persian by Alireza Abiz

The first time I heard the word 'exile' was when my grandmother narrated the story of the Fall in a poetic voice. The first humans were driven out of Paradise for eating the forbidden fruit and disobeying a tyrannical god. They were sent to a faraway place called earth to live forever in exile, with the pain of homesickness, yearning to return to the primordial heaven.

Later, when I learned the poems of Ferdowsi's *Shahnameh*, legends and mythology, the word assumed new meanings. Concepts such as 'separation', 'being driven out of one's birthplace', 'being away from one's motherland', 'enthusiasm for adventure', 'knowledge', 'rebellion' and 'punishment' stood side by side in my mind and I discovered that exile and separation, just like love and birth and death, are amongst the oldest topics which have inspired poets and writers.

As I learned to read and write, exile became a more tangible concept for me. There was a bookseller in our neighbourhood who was also a poet and a political activist. He used to lend us children rare and forbidden books. This was our shared secret. After a while his shop, which was no more than a kiosk with a small glass window, was closed down. We didn't hear from him for a long time. Much later, we heard he had been sent to a faraway town as an alternative punishment to prison. A place far from his bookshelves and the familiar alleyways, where he had no friend or acquaintance. A place so alien that he had no right to leave and return home, where he was confined without any chains on his feet. A city called exile.

At eight, I was forced to leave my beautiful childhood house and its delightful garden. I was permanently separated from my mother to live with my father and his new wife, a Turkish-speaking lady from Azerbaijan, in a suburban neighbourhood. I placed all my belongings – a few sets of clothes and some story books – in a small suitcase, and hid my longing for my mother and my playmates in there too. This incident changed the meaning of 'separation' for me, from an idea to a lived experience. I was so young that I had neither the courage to protest nor the ability to escape. Only the poems and stories that my stepmother told me created a bond of understanding between us, and I gradually managed to overcome the fear of estrangement and loneliness.

Years later, during the early days of my immigration to Sweden, I remembered those childhood days and my innocent efforts both to accept and to be accepted in my new environment. I was 43 when, on a snowy morning, I remembered what I had learned from being in the same position all those years ago. An experience which drove me toward writing poetry and fiction.

Everything that I had left behind – the adventures of my adolescence during the 1979 Iranian revolution, the eight-year Iraq-Iran war, my becoming a mother in the prime of youth, being banned from teaching and forced to stay home, and the memories of my dear friends who were jailed, executed, or fled Iran – awoke in me like wounded recollections as I found myself far away from my homeland. In the solitude of migration, the faded images of years and the voices of shadows appeared in my dreams, thoughts and internal monologues like an alter ego. They walked with me and my poems in every new city, so that I could have a listener.

Now I was able to watch myself, my books, and whatever I had written amidst all the violence and dominant censorship, from a distance. I remembered how my generation faced the monster of suffocating tyranny and despotism in their daily lives. How most of my artist, writer, and journalist friends had fought this monster on a daily basis with thousands of tactics and techniques. How some of them were killed in order that we may not forget the beautiful face of freedom and happiness.

I must confess that while I was brimming with invaluable experiences in my new environment, I felt like a disoriented runner faced with hundreds of questions mixed with hope and disappointment, not knowing which direction to take. Once again, it was the regenerative force of memories, my enthusiasm for storytelling and discovering new words to express myself, which came to my rescue and motivated me to strive.

Cloudy skies, unfamiliar faces, and alleyways which didn't lead me to any friend's home became kind and familiar as soon as I wrote about them in my native language. They were reborn in my poems in a shape that I could claim ownership of.

In the poetry, culture, and history of every land there is a magic force of parallel mirrors which take us on a tour of self-discovery in a fantastical space. By reading Swedish poetry, I stepped into the picturesque labyrinth of a new land, line by line. I experienced common human feelings in the poems of Gunnar Ekelöf, Edith Södergran, Karin Boye and others. Deep and intimate emotions which saved me from the feelings of isolation and oblivion.

Two great exiled poets, Dante Alighieri and Jalāl-al-Din Rumi, are to me the epitome and embodiment of facing the tragedies of war, displacement and the loss of homeland and companions. These two poets, living during a similar period but on two different continents, both spent their lives fleeing massacre and destruction, seeking light in the darkest time. Their stunning allegorical descriptions of the physical and spiritual hardships they endured along the way have become a lasting legacy for all future generations. And both poets describe in their work a return towards the divine, towards love, and away from separation.

The quest for love, beauty and wisdom in Dante's *Divine Comedy*, a spiritual journey to the inferno, purgatory and paradise, ultimately culminates in a favourable outcome: an encounter with the divine essence in paradise.

As a young boy, Rumi was compelled to leave his birthplace of Balkh along with his family due to the Mongol invasion. After a lengthy journey, he eventually settled in the city of Konya among the Turkish-speaking people on the distant fringes of the Seljuk territories. The mesmerising romantic ghazals and the profound wisdom in his *The Mathnawi* are inspired by the human pain of separation and yearning for reunion. We Iranians view him as a poet-philosopher who believed love to be the meaning and purpose of life and for whom the greatest mystical quest was the path toward the truth of the universe. For Rumi, the only way to be saved from isolation and to return to the origin is to experience reunion in love.

In Rumi's poetry, separation of time-bound humans from the boundlessness of God, separation of lover from the beloved, and separation from motherland are three symbolic situations in human life wherein the concepts of separation and exile are sublimated into a mystical code in the pursuit of perfection.

For example, in the introduction to *The Mathnawi* he writes:

> Listen
> as this reed
> pipes its plaint
> unfolds its tale
> of separations:
> Cut from my reedy bed

my crying
ever since
makes men and women
weep.[1]

Forced displacement, or being driven out of ancestral lands due to war, natural disasters or aggressive rulers have had a very profound and symbolic impact on Persian classical poetry and prose, and have arguably led to the development of new styles in poetry. Exile is a journey that starts by leaving the homeland but leads to discovery of the unknown. It is a path trodden with hardship and suffering but it moulds you into a new human being through spiritual and cognitive blossoming.

In the contemporary world, alongside natural disasters, wars and revolutions, one of the most significant motivations for the migration of intellectuals and artists has been the protest against political and social conditions, and resistance against autocracy, censorship and oppression. Migrant literature, the cultural diaspora, and the activities of exiled writers and intellectuals are first and foremost influenced by this perseverance in the struggle for freedom. Poets who are forced to leave their homeland to be a voice against oppression, violence, and censorship live in the sphere of two places and two times, navigating the complexities of their dual existence.

The struggle of the exiled poet, fuelled by the desire for an end to tyranny in their homeland mixed with the hope of their eventual return, carries a nostalgic yet defiant tone. Their resistance, which takes shape with new ideas, has the potential to create new perspectives in one's poetic language through knowledge of the world and new cultures. In this way it becomes a vehicle for expression of shared human aspirations, bridging multiple cultures.

1   Translated by Franklin D. Lewis, taken from his *Rumi – Past and Present, East and West: The Life, Teaching and Poetry of Jalâl al-Din Rumi* (Oneworld Publications).

However, amidst all of this, there is always a dark abyss in the mundanity of the tumultuous world of politics, that pulls the forces of imagination, innovation and artistic rebellion into itself. This abyss has the power to exhaust even the most intellectually apt, dynamic and daring artists, driving them into seclusion or relegating them to the fringes. Struggling with learning a new language, the unfamiliarity of cultural and social dynamics, or simply the ache of estrangement, poets may find themselves ensnared in countless conflicts. This relentless and complicated current ultimately strangles the opportunity to absorb and creatively reinterpret personal experiences and discoveries.

This is where translation and publishing organisations, literary journals, and the supporting cultural foundations play a vital role in supporting poets. They provide an opportunity for writers to connect and engage with the host society and with each other, allowing diverse cultural branches to flourish, bloom and remain vibrant side by side.

Through my own experience, I have observed that there exists an unspoken expectation for an exiled artist to solely reiterate the limited information heard on the political news headlines and confirm stereotypical narratives about their homeland. Yet we all know that such cursory knowledge cannot be representative of a culture, a history, a language, and the intellectual life of a nation. An exiled poet or artist embodies more than just a geographical boundary and a political setting. Through their work, they can introduce a world with thousands of secrets, marvels, and the profundity of cultural manifestations. They can share the experiences of centuries of human endeavours, tell untold stories of love, hope and beauty, and offer a different way to look at and think about life. What poetry creates is the expression of sorrows and joys, emotions and aspirations which are common to all human beings. Similarities that, through empathy, bring us closer together and don't allow national and geographical differences, political and ideological bigotries, or the despotic forces of power and violence to divide us.

Long live poetry and the poets who, in every language, are the true heirs of love, wisdom, and enlightenment.

The Authors

AL-SADDIQ AL-RADDI is one of the leading African poets writing in Arabic today. He is the author of three collections in Arabic: *Songs of Solitude* (1996), *The Sultan's Labyrinth* (1996) and *The Far Reaches of the Screen...* (1999). His poems in English translation have been published in the *Poetry Review* and the *Times Literary Supplement*, among others. His landmark poem 'Poem of the Nile' was published in the *London Review of Books* and later added to the permanent collection of London's Petrie Museum of Egyptian Archaeology, where Al-Raddi spent time as poet-in-residence during the summer of 2012. With the Poetry Translation Centre he has published *He Tells Tales of Meroe* (2015), *A Monkey at the Window* (2016, co-published with Bloodaxe Books) and *A Friend's Kitchen* (2023).

DIANA ANPHIMIADI is a poet, publicist, linguist and teacher. She has published four collections of poetry: *Shokoladi* (*Chocolate*, 2008), *Konspecturi Mitologia* (*Notes on Mythology*, 2009), *Alhlokhedvis Traektoria* (*Trajectory of the Short-Sighted*, 2012) and *Chrdilis Amoch'ra* (*Cutting the Shadow*, 2015). Her poetry has received prestigious awards, including first prize in the 2008 Tsero (Crane) literary contest and the Saba literary award for best first collection in 2009. With the Poetry Translation Centre she has published *Beginning to Speak* (2018) and *Why I No Longer Write Poems* (2022, co-published with Bloodaxe Books), both translated by Natalia Bukia-Peters in collaboration with the poet Jean Sprackland. Diana Anphimiadi lives in Tbilisi with her son.

DIANA BELLESSI was born in Zavalla, Argentina, in 1946. She is considered to be the godmother of LGBTQI+ poetry in Argentina. Her poetry, prose and translation work spans four decades, and demonstrates a deep commitment to progressive politics, ecological conservation and the social condition of the working class in Latin America. She has received a Guggenheim Fellowship for poetry, a fellowship from the Fundación Antorchas, a Diploma of Merit from the Fundación Konex, Spain's Melilla International Poetry Prize and Argentina's National Poetry Prize. With the Poetry Translation Centre she has published *To Love a Woman* (2022), translated by Leo Boix.

CARLA DIACOV is a Brazilian poet and artist born in the state of São Paulo in 1975. She has published various books of poetry, including *Amanhã alguém morre no samba* (*Tomorrow someone dies in the samba*) (2015). She also maintains a prolific online output of poetry, photography, videos and visual art, including paintings using her own menstrual blood. Thanks to this, her playfully avant-garde, viscerally political work has developed a cult following both inside and outside Brazil.

AZITA GHAHREMAN was born in Mashhad in 1962. One of Iran's leading poets, she has lived in Sweden since 2006. She has published five collections of poetry: *Eve's Songs* (1991), *Sculptures of Autumn* (1995), *Forgetfulness is a Simple Ritual* (2002), *The Suburb of Crows* (2008) and *Under Hypnosis in Dr Caligari's Cabinet* (2012). Her poems have been translated into German, Dutch, Arabic, Chinese, Swedish, French, Russian, Ukrainian, Turkish, Danish and English. She is a member of the South Sweden Writers' Union. In 2018 the Poetry Translation Centre and Bloodaxe Books co-published *Negative of a Group Photograph*, a selection of Ghahreman's poetry translated into English by Elhum Shakerifar with the poet Maura Dooley.

LEGNA RODRÍGUEZ IGLESIAS (Camagüey, 1984) is a prize-winning Cuban poet, fiction writer and playwright. Among her literary awards are the Centrifugados Prize for Younger Poets (Spain, 2019), the Paz Prize (the National Poetry Series, 2017), the Casa de las Américas Prize in Theater (Cuba, 2016) and the Julio Cortázar Ibero-American Short Story Prize (2011). In 2019 the Poetry Translation Centre and Bloodaxe Books co-published a selection of her poetry in English translation under the title *A little body are many parts* (translated by Abigail Parry and Serafina Vick). Her novel *My Favorite Girlfriend Was a French Bulldog* was translated into English by Megan McDowell and published in the USA in 2020 by McSweeneys. She lives in Miami where she writes a column for the online journal *El Estornudo* and *Hypermedia Magazine*.

KARIN KARAKAŞLI was born in Istanbul in 1972. She graduated in Translation and Interpreting Studies. From 1996 to 2006 she worked at the Turkish-Armenian weekly newspaper *Agos* as editor, head of the editorial department and columnist on both Turkish and Armenian pages. She has completed an MA in Comparative Literature, works as a translation instructor at the university and as a teacher of Armenian language and literature in an Armenian High School. She is currently a columnist at *Agos* and *Radikal* newspapers, and continues to write fiction and poetry. She is the author of three poetry collections as well as several short story collections and novels. She is the co-writer of the research book *Türkiye'de Ermeniler: Cemaat, Birey, Yurttaş* (*Armenians in Turkey: Community, Individual, Citizen*). With the Poetry Translation Centre she has published *History–Geography* (2017) and *Real* (2024), both translated by Canan Marasligil in collaboration with the poet Sarah Howe.

KARAN KUROSE was born in Osaka. He is chief priest of the Gannenji Buddhist temple, in Toyama. He studied with the tanka poet Ken Kasugai (1938–2004). He has published four volumes of poetry. He works as a poetry judge for the NHK tanka TV programme, and for the Mirai tanka society.

LEE HYEMI (b. 1988) is the author of three poetry collections and an essay collection. At eighteen, she was one of the youngest winners of the JoongAng Literary Newcomer's Prize. Her second collection *Unexpected Vanilla*, translated into English by Soje, was shortlisted for the 2021 National Translation Award in Poetry and the 2022 Sarah Maguire Prize for Poetry in Translation.

URSULA K LE GUIN (1929–2018) was a celebrated author whose body of work includes 23 novels, twelve volumes of short stories, eleven volumes of poetry, thirteen children's books, five essay collections, and four works of translation. The breadth and imagination of her work earned her six Nebula Awards, seven Hugo Awards, and SFWA's Grand Master, along with the PEN/ Malamud and many other awards. In 2014 she was awarded the National Book Foundation Medal for Distinguished Contribution to American Letters, and in 2016 joined the short list of authors to be published in their lifetimes by the Library of America.

BEJAN MATUR is the most illustrious poet among a bold new women's poetry emerging from the Middle East. Her poetry has been translated into 43 languages, and has won numerous awards. She has published eleven books, nine of which are poetry, and has performed her work all over the world. Her second collection in English translation, *How Abraham Abandoned Me*, translated by Ruth Christie with Selçuk Berilgen (Arc, 2012) was the Poetry Book Society's Translation Choice for Spring 2012. With the Poetry Translation Centre she has published *Akin to Stone* (2020), translated by Canan Marasligil with the poet Jen Hadfield. Bejan Matur is a graduate of the Ankara University Faculty of Law, and currently lives between Berlin and Istanbul.

GABRIEL *MWÈNÈ* OKOUNDJI was born in Okondo-Ewo, Republic of Congo, in 1962. He lives in Bordeaux, practising as a clinical psychologist, having received a Congolese government grant to carry out his higher education in France. Encounters with Occitan writers inspired his poetry, and Occitan was the first language in which he was published. Often incorporating untranslated words and phrases into his work, Okoundji prefers to describe himself as a *passeur* (intermediary or ferryman) than as a poet, with a mission to transport words, proverbs, stories, and voices from his mother tongue, Teke, towards 'the universal'.

MOHAN RANA (b. 1964) is a Hindi poet who grew up and studied in Delhi and now lives in Bath, England. He writes poems exploring themes of identity, truth, memories and nature. He has published ten poetry collections in Hindi. With the Poetry Translation Centre he has published *The Cartographer* (2020), translated by Lucy Rosenstein with the poet Bernard O'Donoghue.

HABIB TENGOUR is one of the leading visionary writers of postcolonial Algeria. Rooted in Maghribi cultural identity and memory, his poems consider the experience of exile in a voice that is by turns unsentimental and surreal. He has published more than 15 works of poetry, prose, theatre and essays, and his work has been translated into English, German, Arabic, Italian, Macedonian and Dutch. He has also translated poets from other languages into French, for example Pierre Joris, Hans Thill and Saadi Youssef. In 2016 he won the Dante European Poetry Prize for his poetry, and in 2022 he was awarded the Prix Benjamin Fondane for the entire body of his work. With the Poetry Translation Centre he has published *Consolatio* (2022), translated by Will Harris and Delaina Haslam.

VICTOR TERÁN was born in Juchitán de Zaragoza in 1958. His work has been published extensively in magazines and anthologies throughout Mexico. His books of poetry include *Sica ti Gubidxa Cubi* (Editorial Diana, 1994) and *Ca Guichi Xtí' Guendaranaxhii* (Editorial Praxis, 2003). With the Poetry Translation Centre he has published *Poems* (2010), translated by Shook. Victor Terán works as a media education teacher at the secondary level, on the Oaxacan Isthmus.

XASAN DAAHIR ISMAACIIL 'WEEDHSAME' is recognised as one of the foremost contemporary Somali poets. He has composed over 80 lengthy poems and created more than 75 songs performed by diverse Somali singers. He was mentored by Maxamed Xaashi Dhamac 'Gaarriye', one of the most important Somali poets of any period, with whom he delved into the intricacies of Somali literature, exploring the nuances of Somali prosody, figurative language, and rhetoric. He now teaches Somali literature and Statistics at the University of Hargeysa, and works with the Somaliland Exam Board. Weedhsame's seminal poem 'Galiilyo' was translated into English by Martin Orwin with the poet Daljit Nagra and published as an illustrated poster by the Poetry Translation Centre in 2017; translations of his work also appear in *So At One With You*, an anthology of Somali poetry edited by W.N. Herbert and Said Jama Hussein (The Poetry Translation Centre / Redsea Publications, 2018).

LAURA WITTNER is an award-winning poet and translator from Argentina. Her books of poetry include *El pasillo del tren* (1996), *Los cosacos* (1998), *Las últimas mudanzas* (2001), *La tomadora de café* (2005), *Lluvias* (2009), *Balbuceos en una misma dirección* (2011), *La altura* (2016), *Lugares donde una no está* (2017) and *Traducción de la ruta* (2020), whose English edition (*Translation of the Route*, translated by Juana Adcock) is co-published by the Poetry Translation Centre and Bloodaxe Books in 2024. She has also published more than 20 books for children, most recently *Cual para tal* (2022), *¿Y comieron perdices?* (2023) and *Se pide un deseo* (2023). As a literary translator Wittner has translated books by Leonard Cohen, David Markson, M. John Harrison, Cynan Jones, Claire-Louise Bennett, Katherine Mansfield and James Schuyler, among many others.

YANG LIAN was one of the original Misty Poets who reacted against the strictures of the Cultural Revolution. His work was criticised in China in 1983 and formally banned in 1989 when he organised memorial services for the dead of Tiananmen while in New Zealand. He was a Chinese poet in exile from 1989 to 1995, and now lives in Berlin. Translations of his poetry include *Where the Sea Stands Still* (1999), *Yi* (2002), *Concentric Circles* (2005), Lee *Valley Poems* (2009), *Narrative Poem* (2017), *A Tower Built Downwards* (2023), and *Anniversary Snow* (2019) which won the 2020 Sarah Maguire Prize for Poetry in Translation. He was awarded the International Nonino Prize in 2012.

YU YOYO was born in Sichuan in 1990, and has been writing poetry since 2004. Works include the poetry collections *Seven Years*, *Me as Bait*, *Wind Can't*, *Half a Person* and *A Cat is a Cloud*; the short story collection *Nonexistent Cat*; and *A Person Newly Blind*, an art installation. Her poems have been used in drama, painting, music, photography and film, and translated into multiple languages, including Korean, Russian, French, Japanese, Swedish, and Arabic. With the Poetry Translation Centre she has published *My Tenantless Body* (2019), translated by Dave Haysom with the poet AK Blakemore.

ASHA LUL MOHAMUD YUSUF is regarded as one of the most outstanding Somali poets of her generation. Although she has lived in exile in the UK for 20 years, through recordings, TV and the internet her poems are well-known among Somalis both at home and abroad. A powerful woman poet in a literary tradition still largely dominated by men, Asha Lul is a master of the major Somali poetic forms, including the prestigious gabay which presents compelling arguments with mesmerising feats of alliteration. Her first collection in English translation, *The Sea-Migrations* (The Poetry Translation Centre/Bloodaxe Books, 2018), was translated by Maxamed Xasan 'Alto' and Said Jama Hussein with the poet Clare Pollard, and named Poetry Book of the Year by *The Sunday Times*.

ZAR MOSE is a writer, poet, and digital imaging artist born and raised in Batusangkar, West Sumatra, currently pursuing a bachelor's degree in English literature at Diponegoro University, Semarang. He is the author of *Galeri Hormonal* (One Peach Media,

2021). His works consistently explore queerness in poz, Minang-kabau, and Abrahamic religion landscapes.

ÉRICA ZÍNGANO (Fortaleza, 1980) is a poet and researcher, who also works with visual and performance arts. She currently lives in Fortaleza and is a PhD candidate in Comparative Literature with a special focus on contemporary Brazilian literature at the Federal University of Ceará. Her publications include *fio, fenda, falésia* (2010), in collaboration with Renata Huber and Roberta Ferraz, funded by the São Paulo Secretary for Culture ProAc-2009 programme; *Ich weiß nicht warum – Zeichnungen und Texte für Unica Zürn* (2013), a dual-language edition translated into German by Odile Kennel and published by hochroth berlin; and the collective book *eine Sache für eine andere* (2017), written in collaboration with Lotto Thießen, Nathalie Quintane, Marion Breton, Rob Packer, Odile Kennel, Mercedes M. and Marília Garcia – written and translated into non-native languages, by the australian publisher bulky news press. Zíngano has also been featured in anthologies of Brazilian poetry, including *Uma alegria estilhaçada* (2019), curated by Gustavo Ribeiro and *As 29 poetas Hoje* (2021), edited by Heloísa Buarque de Holanda. She also writes essays and criticism.

The Translators

ALIREZA ABIZ is a multi-award-winning Iranian poet, literary scholar, and translator. He has written extensively on Persian contemporary literature and culture. His book *Censorship of Literature in Post-Revolutionary Iran: Politics and Culture Since 1979* was published by Bloomsbury in 2020. He has published five collections of poetry in Persian, including *Black Line, London Underground* (winner of the 2018 Shamlou Poetry Award) and has translated the poetry of Rainer Maria Rilke, Basil Bunting, Derek Walcott, Allen Ginsberg, C.K. Williams and others into Persian. Translations of his poetry have been published in numerous journals and anthologies. A selection of his poetry in English translation titled *The Kindly Interrogator* was published by Shearsman in 2021.

ATEF ALSHAER is a Senior Lecturer in Arabic Studies at the University of Westminster. He has been an active translator with the Poetry Translation Centre since 2008. His publications include *Poetry and Politics in the Modern Arab World* (2016), *A Map of Absence: An Anthology of Palestinian Writing on the Nakba* (2019), and the edited volume *Love and Poetry in the Middle East: Literature from Antiquity to the Present* (2022).

LEO BOIX is a bilingual Latinx poet born in Argentina and based in the UK. His debut collection in English, *Ballad of a Happy Immigrant*, was published by Chatto & Windus in 2021 and was a Poetry Book Society Wild Card Choice. Boix is a fellow of The Complete Works programme and a board member of *Magma Poetry*. He is also a co-director of Un Nuevo Sol, an Arts Council England-supported scheme that aims to promote Latinx writers in the UK. Boix has received several awards for his poetry, including the Bart Wolffe Poetry Award, the Keats-Shelley Prize and a PEN Award. He is the translator of Diana Bellessi's *To Love a Woman* (Poetry Translation Centre, 2022).

NATALIA BUKIA-PETERS is a freelance translator, interpreter and teacher of Georgian and Russian. She studied at Ilia'sTbilisi State University and she has an MA in Russian and Eurasian Studies at Leiden University, the Netherlands. She is a member of the Chartered Institute of Linguists in London and has worked collaboratively with the Poetry Translation Centre since 2013. Her translations have been published both in the UK (Fal Publications, Francis Boutle, Bloodaxe Books) and USA (Dalkey Archive). Her most recent poetry books are Diana Anphimiadi's *Why I No Longer Write Poems* (Poetry Translation Centre / Bloodaxe Books), translated in collaboration with Jean Sprackland; and Lia Sturua's *On the Contrary* (Fal Publications), in collaboration with Victoria Field.

DR ALAN CUMMINGS is Senior Lecturer in Japanese Studies at SOAS University of London. His research interests include kabuki dramaturgy and post-war performance. Recent publications include *Haiku: Love* (2013), and 'Money is all that matters in the world' in Jones & Watanabe (eds.), *A Tokyo Anthology: Literature from Japan's Modern Metropolis 1850–1920* (2017).

SARABJEET GARCHA is a poet, editor, translator and publisher. His five books of poems include *All We Have* and *A Clock in the Far Past*, in addition to a volume each of poems translated from Marathi and prose translated from Hindi. He has translated several American poets into Hindi, including W.S. Merwin and John Haines, and several Indian poets into English, among them Mangalesh Dabral and Leeladhar Jagoori. His poems, translations and essays have been published in the *Notre Dame Review*, *Versopolis*, *Lyrikline*, *Modern Poetry in Translation*, *Asymptote*, *Two Lines Journal*, the *Indian Quarterly*, *Scroll*, the *Wire*, among other publications and several anthologies. He has received the Fellowship for Outstanding Artists from the Government of

India, the International Publishing Fellowship from the British Council, and the inaugural Godyo Podyo Probondho Award. His poems have been translated into German, Spanish, Russian, Malayalam, Kannada, Marathi, Punjabi and Hindi.

DELAINA HASLAM specialises in the field of sociology, translating for French universities and academic journals. With a keen interest in literary translation, she did the British Centre for Literary Translation Summer School in 2016, which led to invaluable collaborations and a series of Poetry Translation Centre workshops on francophone African poets. The PTC published her co-translations with Will Harris of the work of Algerian poet Habib Tengour as part of its World Poet Series in 2022.

DAVE HAYSOM has been translating, editing, and writing about contemporary Chinese literature since 2012. Managing editor of *Pathlight* magazine from 2014 to 2018, he has translated novels by Feng Tang, Li Er, and Xu Zechen, in addition to *Nothing But the Now*, a short story collection by Wen Zhen. His essays and reviews have appeared in *Granta*, *Words Without Borders*, *The Millions*, *China Channel* and *SUPChina*, and his portfolio is online at spittingdog.net. In 2019 the Poetry Translation Centre published his co-translation with the poet AK Blakemore of Yu Yoyo's poetry under the title *My Tenantless Body*.

BRIAN HOLTON is a translator and musician from Scotland. He was the first Programme Director of the Chinese-English / English-Chinese translation programme at Newcastle University. He taught translation for ten years at the Hong Kong Polytechnic University and in 1992 he began a continuing working relationship with the poet Yang Lian, which has so far resulted in a dozen books of translated poetry, including *Where the Sea Stands Still* (Bloodaxe Books, 1999), *Concentric Circles* (with Agnes Hung-Chong Chan) (Bloodaxe Books, 2005), *Lee Valley Poems* (with Agnes Hung-Chong Chan and seven poets) (Bloodaxe Books, 2009), *Narrative Poem* (Bloodaxe Books,

2017), *Anniversary Snow* (Shearsman Books, 2019) and *A Tower Built Downwards* (Bloodaxe Books, 2023). He is the lead translator and associate editor of *Jade Ladder: Contemporary Chinese Poetry* (Bloodaxe Books, 2012). He also translates into Scots and is the only currently-publishing Chinese-Scots translator in the world. His latest Chinese-Scots translations are *Hard Roads an Cauld Hairst Winds: Li Bai and Du Fu in Scots* (Taproot Press, 2022) and *Aa Cled Wi Clouds She Cam: Saxty Sang Lyrics* (Irish Pages, 2022).

WILL HOWARD's writing and translations have appeared in *Poetry*, *Brevity*, *DIAGRAM*, *Passages North*, *The Offing*, *The Riveter*, and elsewhere. He lives in Madrid.

KHAIRANI BAROKKA is a writer and artist from Jakarta with over two decades of professional translation experience. Okka's work has been presented widely internationally, and centres disability justice as anticolonial praxis, and access as translation. Among her honours, she has been *Modern Poetry in Translation* magazine's Inaugural Poet-in-Residence, a UNFPA Indonesian Young Leader Driving Social Change, and Associate Artist at the UK's National Centre for Writing. Okka's poetry collections include *Ultimatum Orangutan* (2021), shortlisted for the Barbellion Prize, and *amuk* (2024), a book which charts the profound mistranslation of this word (both published by Nine Arches Press).

ANNIE McDERMOTT is the translator of a dozen books from Spanish and Portuguese into English, by such writers as Mario Levrero, Selva Almada, Brenda Lozano and Lídia Jorge. In 2022, she was awarded the Premio Valle-Inclán for her translation of *Wars of the Interior* by Joseph Zárate. She has previously lived in Mexico and Brazil, and is now based in Hastings, in the UK.

MARTIN ORWIN is associate professor at the University of Naples 'L'Orientale' where he teaches and researches Somali language and literature. His research centres on the use of language in poetry and he has written articles on metre, alliteration, Somali poetry as lyric poetry and some analyses of famous poems. He also has an interest in the performance poetry and has published on the relation between language and music. He has worked with the Poetry Translation Centre since its beginning and has published translations of both early and contemporary Somali poetry in various journals and books.

SHOOK is a poet, translator, and filmmaker raised in Mexico City. In their debut collection, *Our Obsidian Tongues* (2013), Shook explores the violence and hunger of everyday life. They have translated over 15 books from Spanish and Isthmus Zapotec, and co-translated Al-Saddiq Al-Raddi's *A Friend's Kitchen* (2023) from the Arabic in collaboration with Bryar Bajalan.

SOJE (b. 1994) is a poet and the translator of Lee Hyemi's *Unexpected Vanilla* (Tilted Axis Press, 2020), Lee Soho's *Catcalling* (Open Letter Books, 2021), and Choi Jin-young's *To the Warm Horizon* (Honford Star, 2021). They also make *chogwa*, a zine that features one Korean poem and multiple English translations per issue.

AYÇA TÜRKOĞLU is a literary translator working from German and Turkish. Her work has been shortlisted for the 2022 Helen & Kurt Wolff Translator's Prize and longlisted for the Warwick Women in Translation Prize. She lives in north London.

SERAFINA VICK is a literary translator from Spanish and French. Along with her co-translator Abigail Parry, she won a PEN Translates Award for their translation of Legna Rodríguez Iglesias's selected poems, *A little body are many parts* (Poetry Translation Centre / Bloodaxe Books, 2019). The book was also shortlisted for the Premio Valle Inclán for Spanish Translation and the Derek Walcott Prize for Poetry. Serafina Vick continues to translate and is currently honing her craft as a writer on a

MA in Creative Writing at Bath Spa University. She lives with her Cuban-British family in Wiltshire.

FRANCISCO VILHENA is an editor and translator. He writes short essays and translates from the Portuguese; his co-translation (with Rachel Long) of Adelaide Ivánova's *the hammer and other poems* was shortlisted for the 2020 Derek Walcott Prize for Poetry. His work can be found in *Granta*, *Modern Poetry in Translation*, *Asymptote* and elsewhere. His cat is one of the first feline polyglots.

The Editor

ERICA HESKETH is a Japanese-Danish poet based in London. She has been the Director of the Poetry Translation Centre since 2016. Previous roles include Writers in Translation programme manager at the writers' organisation English PEN, literary events programmer at Southbank Centre, and editor at Bloomsbury Publishing.

The Poetry Translation Centre

Established in 2004, the Poetry Translation Centre is the only UK organisation dedicated to translating, publishing and promoting contemporary poetry from Africa, Asia and Latin America. We introduce extraordinary poets from around the world to new audiences through books, workshops, online resources and dual-language events. We champion diversity and representation in the arts, and work closely with diaspora communities in the UK for whom poetry is of great importance.

The PTC is home to the acclaimed World Poet Series, pocket-sized editions which offer an introduction to some of the world's most exciting contemporary poets to English-speaking readers. Since 2014 we have also published regular standalone collections with Bloodaxe Books, and specialist books on Somali poetry in partnership with Kayd Somali Arts and Culture and Red-Sea Cultural Foundation.

All of our poetry collections are published as dual-language paperback editions. They are available through bookshops in the UK and USA as well as direct from poetrytranslation.org.

A Friend's Kitchen by Al-Saddiq Al-Raddi –
translated from the Arabic by Bryar Bajalan with Shook

This Water by Gagan Gill –
translated from the Hindi by Lucy Rosenstein with Jane Duran

Ask the Thunder by Maxamed Xaashi Dhamac 'Gaarriye' –
translated from the Somali by Martin Orwin with WN Herbert

The Cartographer by Mohan Rana –
translated from the Hindi by Lucy Rosenstein with Bernard O'Donoghue

My Mother's Language by Abdellatif Laâbi –
translated from the French by André Naffis-Sahely

Akin to Stone by Bejan Matur –
translated from the Turkish by Canan Marasligil with Jen Hadfield

the hammer and other poems by Adelaide Ivánova –
translated from the Portuguese by Francisco Vilhena with Rachel Long

My Tenantless Body by Yu Yoyo –
translated from the Chinese by Dave Haysom with AK Blakemore

Aulò! Aulò! Aulò! by Ribka Sibhatu –
translated by André Naffis-Sahely from the Italian and from Italian
translations of the Tigrinya and Amharic made by the author

Embrace by Najwan Darwish –
translated from the Arabic by Atef Alshaer with Paul Batchelor

Leaving by Anar –
translated from the Tamil by Hari Rajaledchumy with Fran Lock

To Love a Woman by Diana Bellessi –
translated from the Spanish by Leo Boix

Consolatio by Habib Tengour –
translated from the French by Will Harris and Delaina Haslam

I Will Not Fold These Maps by Mona Kareem –
translated from the Arabic by Sara Elkamel

CO-PUBLISHED WITH BLOODAXE BOOKS

My Voice: A Decade of Poems from the Poetry Translation Centre –
edited by Sarah Maguire

A Monkey at the Window by Al-Saddiq Al-Raddi –
translated from the Arabic by Atef Alshaer, Rashid El Sheikh, Sabry
Hafez and Hafez Kheir with Sarah Maguire and Mark Ford

The Sea-Migrations by Asha Lul Mohamud Yusuf –
translated from the Somali by Maxamed Xasan 'Alto' and Said Jama
Hussein with Clare Pollard

Negative of a Group Photograph by Azita Ghahreman –
translated from the Persian by Elhum Shakerifar with Maura Dooley

A little body are many parts by Legna Rodríguez Iglesias –
translated from the Spanish by Abigail Parry and Serafina Vick

Why I No Longer Write Poems by Diana Anphimiadi –
translated from the Georgian by Natalia Bukia-Peters with Jean
Sprackland

Translation of the Route by Laura Wittner –
translated from the Spanish by Juana Adcock

CO-PUBLISHED WITH KAYD SOMALI ARTS AND CULTURE
AND RED-SEA CULTURAL FOUNDATION

Hadraawi: The Poet and the Man –
edited by Jama Musse Jama

So At One With You: An Anthology of Modern Poetry in Somali –
edited by WN Herbert and Said Jama Hussein